This book belongs to:

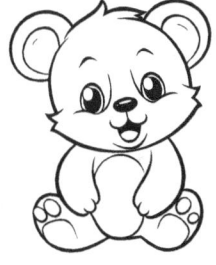
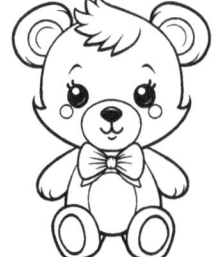

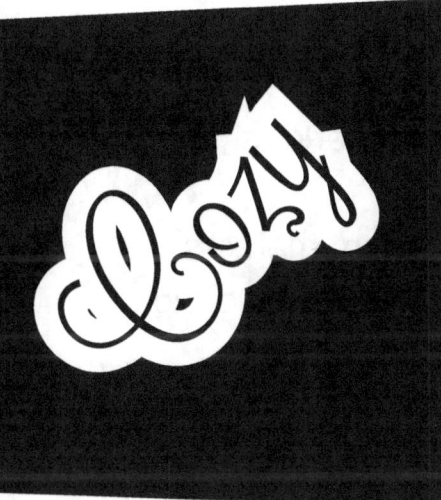
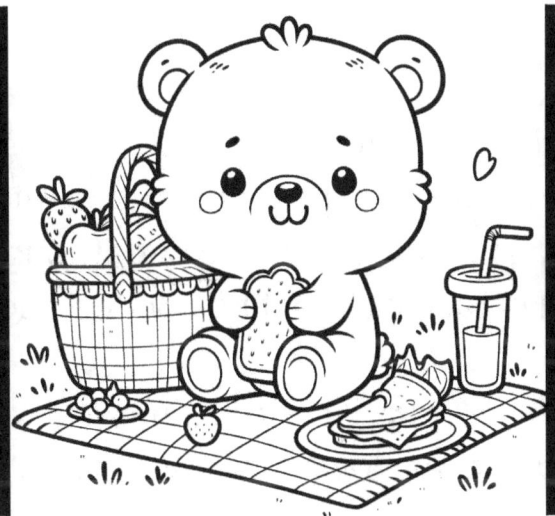
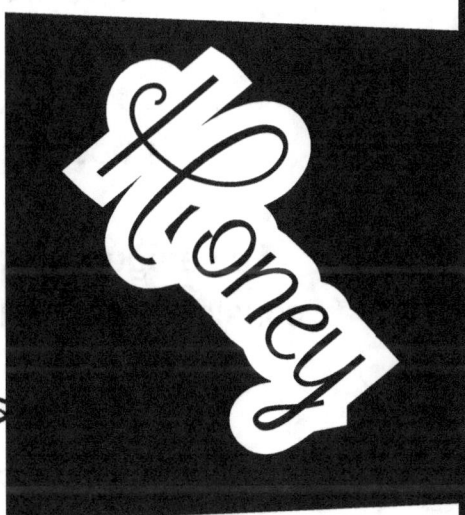

Copyright 2024 ©

Positive Dungeons

No part of this publication may be copied, reproduced in any format, by any means, electronic or otherwise, without prior consent from the copyright owner and publisher of this book.

How to Use This Book

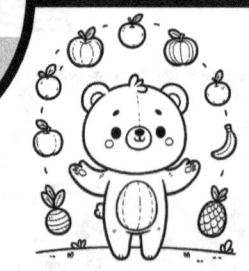
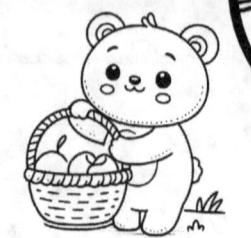

Disconnect from the Outside World
Switch off your phone or put it on airplane mode to enjoy a moment of tranquility and focused immersion.

Prepare Your Space
Choose a comfortable, well-lit space. Consider some soft background music and a relaxing drink to accompany your coloring session.

There Are No Rules in Art
There are no wrong choices in art.
Feel free to experiment with your color palette.

Explore and Experiment
This book is ideally suited for colored pencils or markers.
Please use wet mediums with caution.
To safeguard against any potential bleed-through from markers, consider placing a cardstock sheet behind the page you're coloring.

Practice Mindfulness
Let each stroke guide you toward a meditative state. Concentrate on your hand's movement and how the color fills each space.

Personalize Your Experience
Feel free to add your own details to the illustrations to further personalize your artwork.

Remember, each page of this book is an invitation to explore mythical worlds and rediscover the joy of creating. Happy Coloring!

Share Your Thoughts!
Enjoy Our Bear Coloring Book

Prepare to embark on an adventure into a bear-filled world of wonder with our captivating coloring book. Unleash your imagination as you adorn these pages with lively hues, bringing majestic bears to life! Our aim is to spark joy and creativity within you, and we eagerly anticipate the magnificent artworks you'll create!

GET READY FOR HOURS OF COLORING FUN!

If our coloring book brings smiles to your Life, we'd be grateful for your kind words in a review. Follow the instructions at the end of the book to share your feedback. Your reviews help us continue creating joy-filled experiences for young artists like yours!

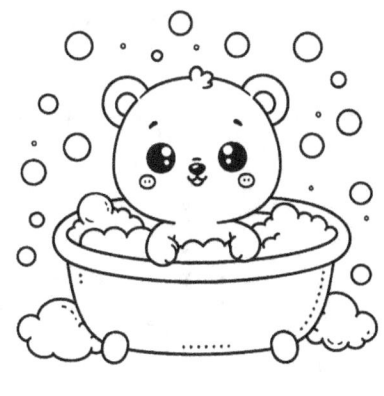

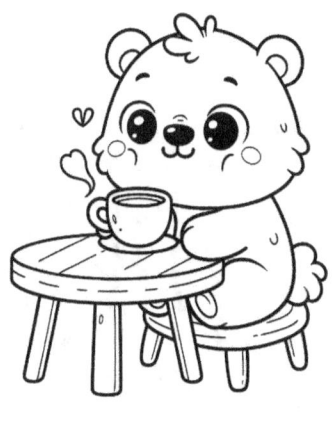

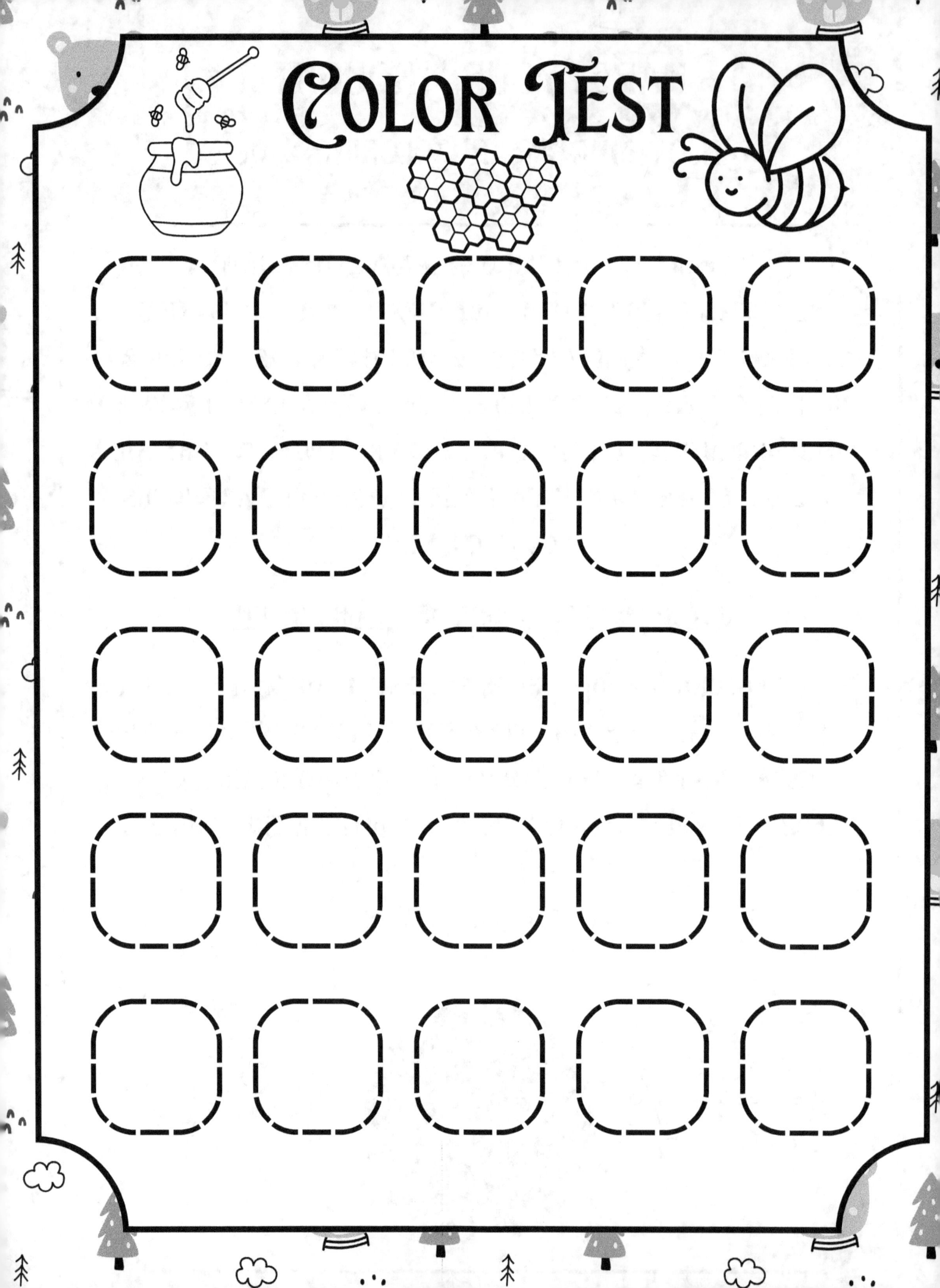

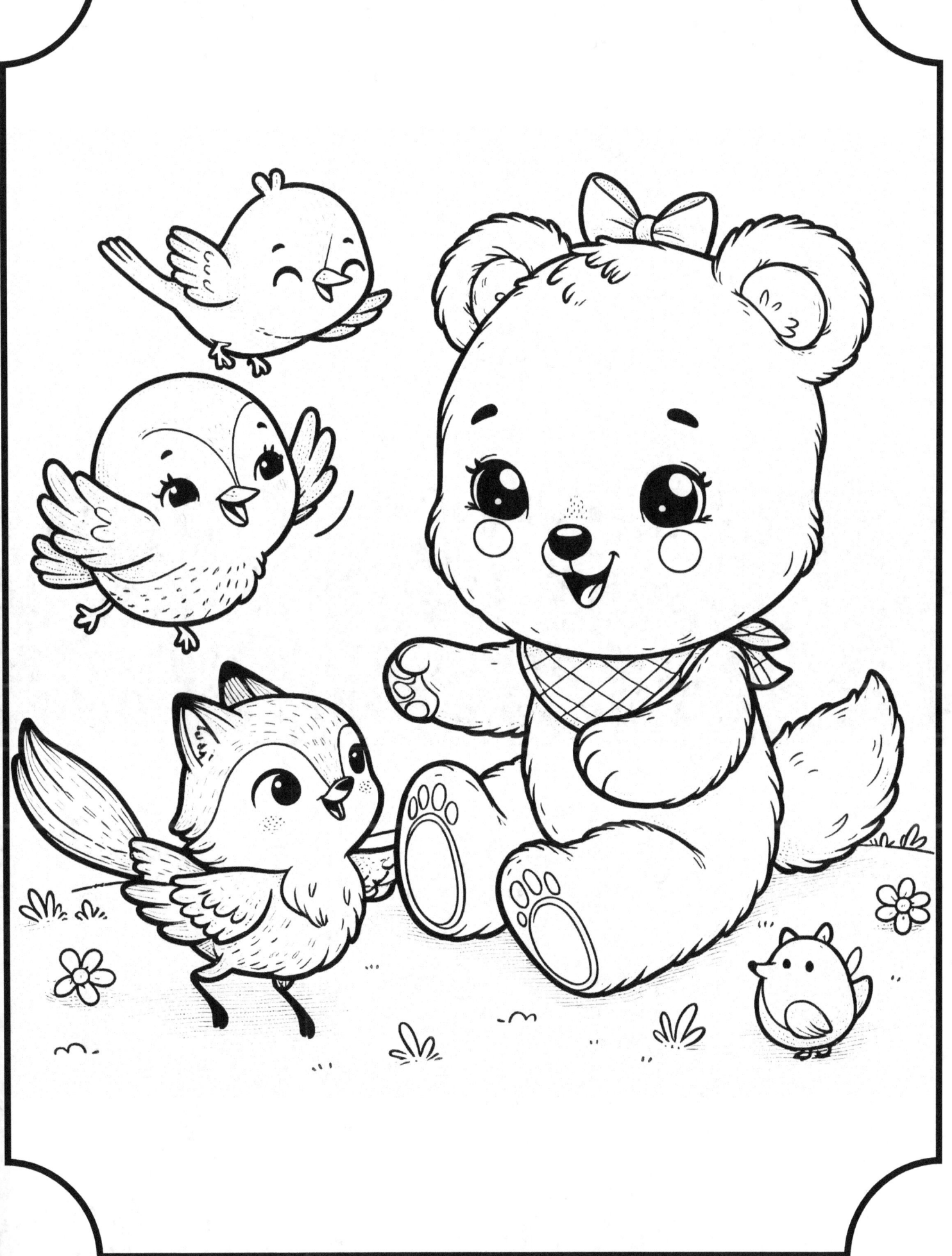

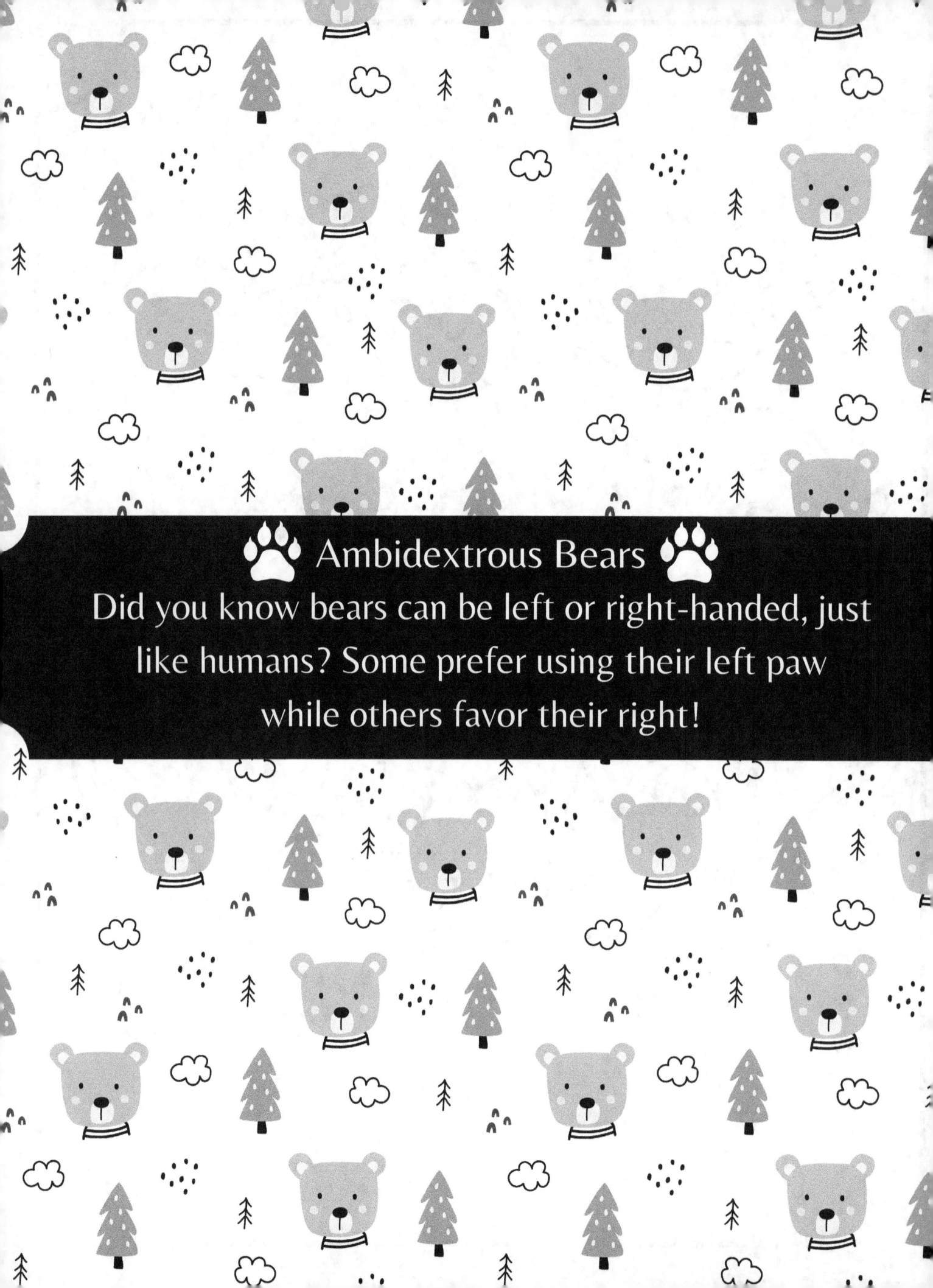

🐾 Ambidextrous Bears 🐾
Did you know bears can be left or right-handed, just like humans? Some prefer using their left paw while others favor their right!

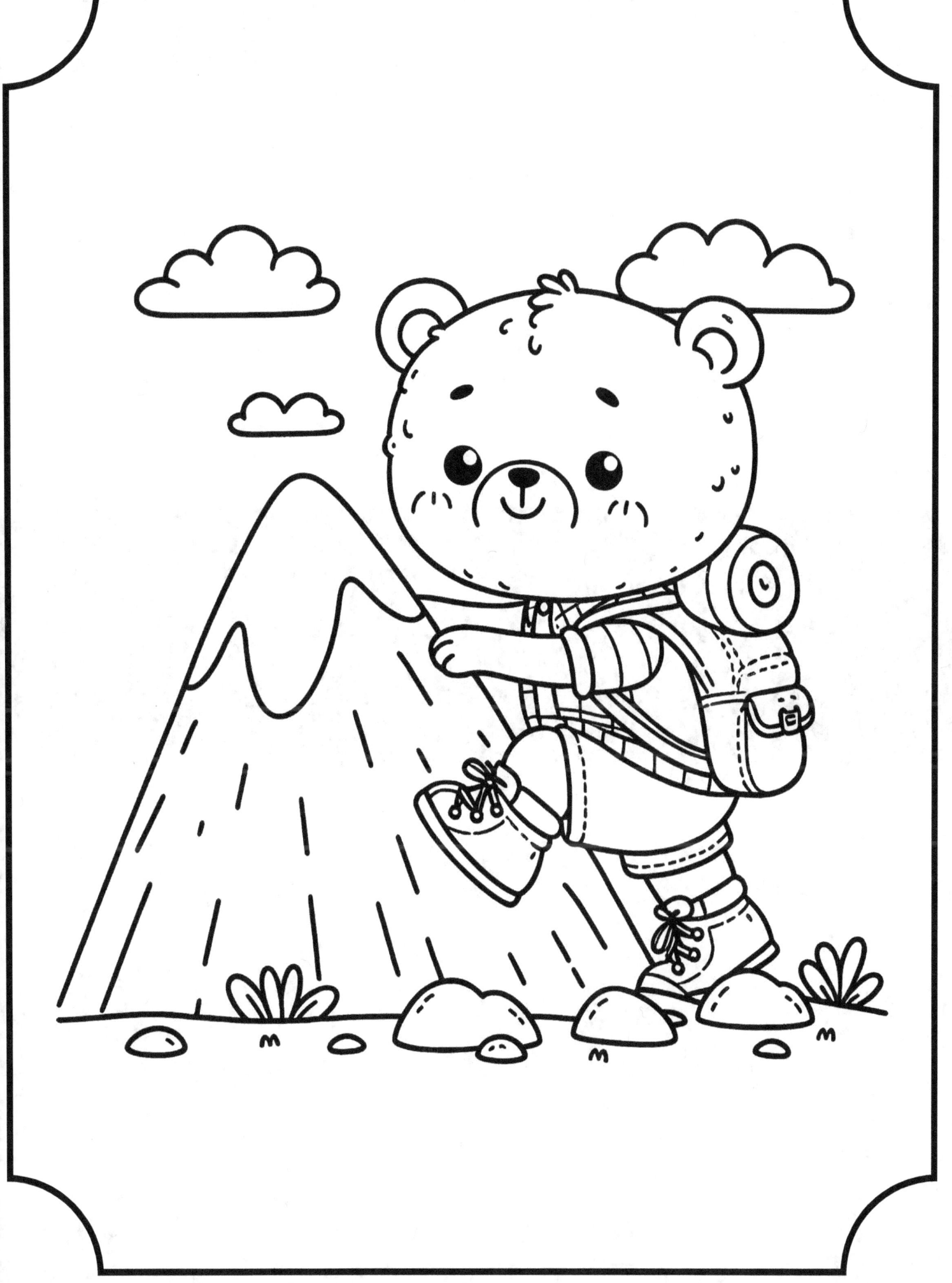

🐾 Super Smellers 🐾
Bears have an incredible sense of smell, which helps them locate food from miles away. It's like having a superpowered nose!

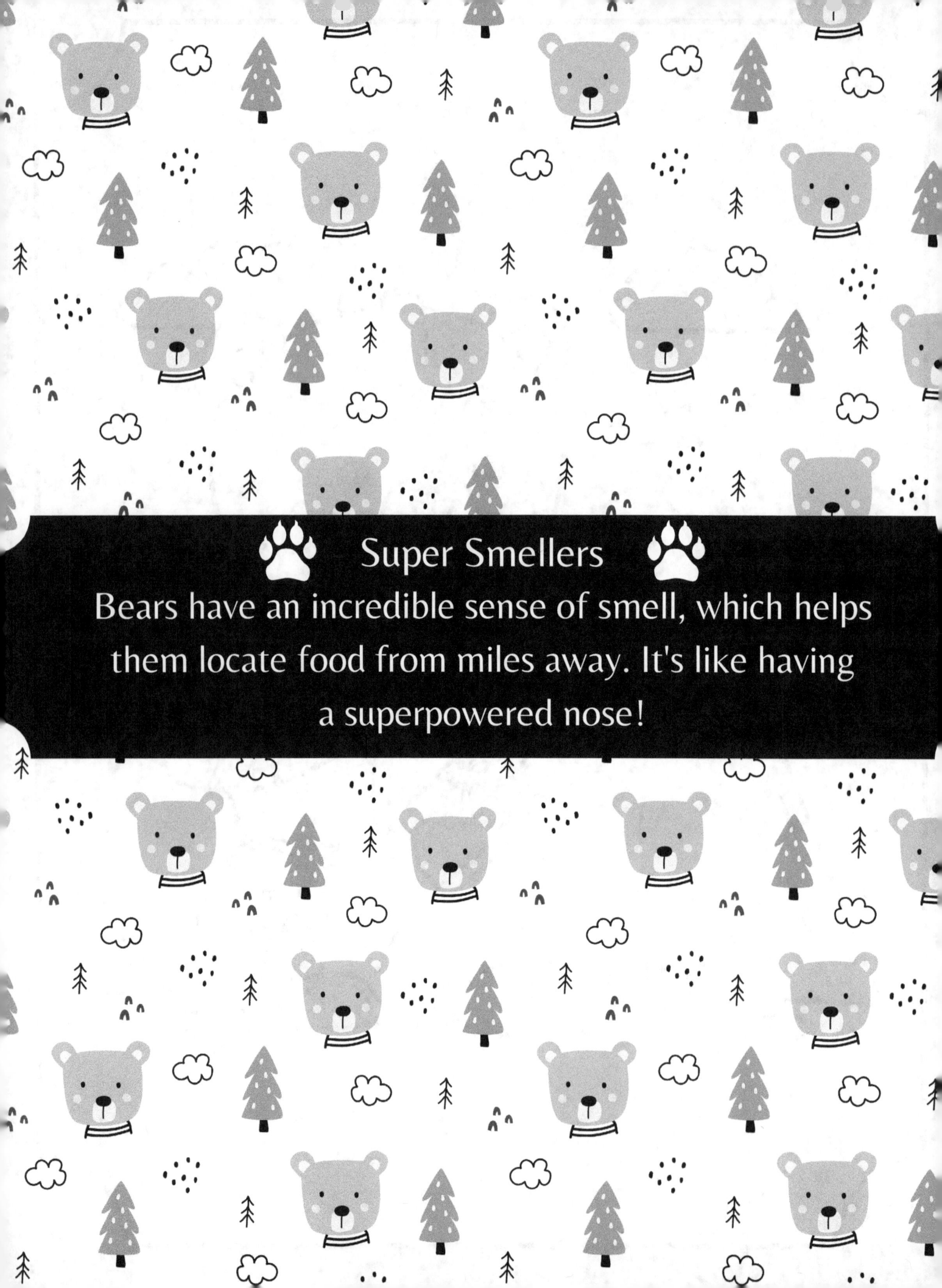

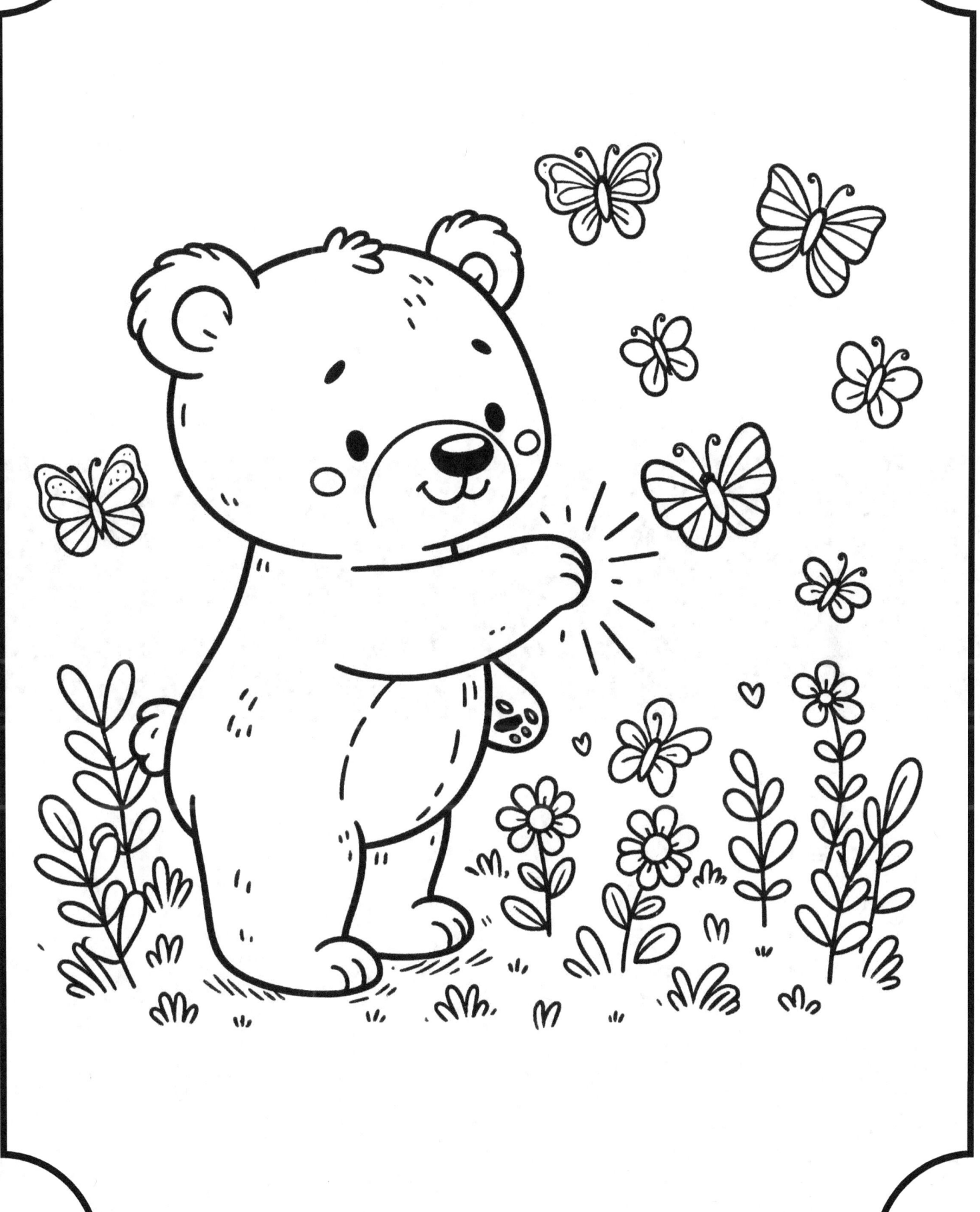

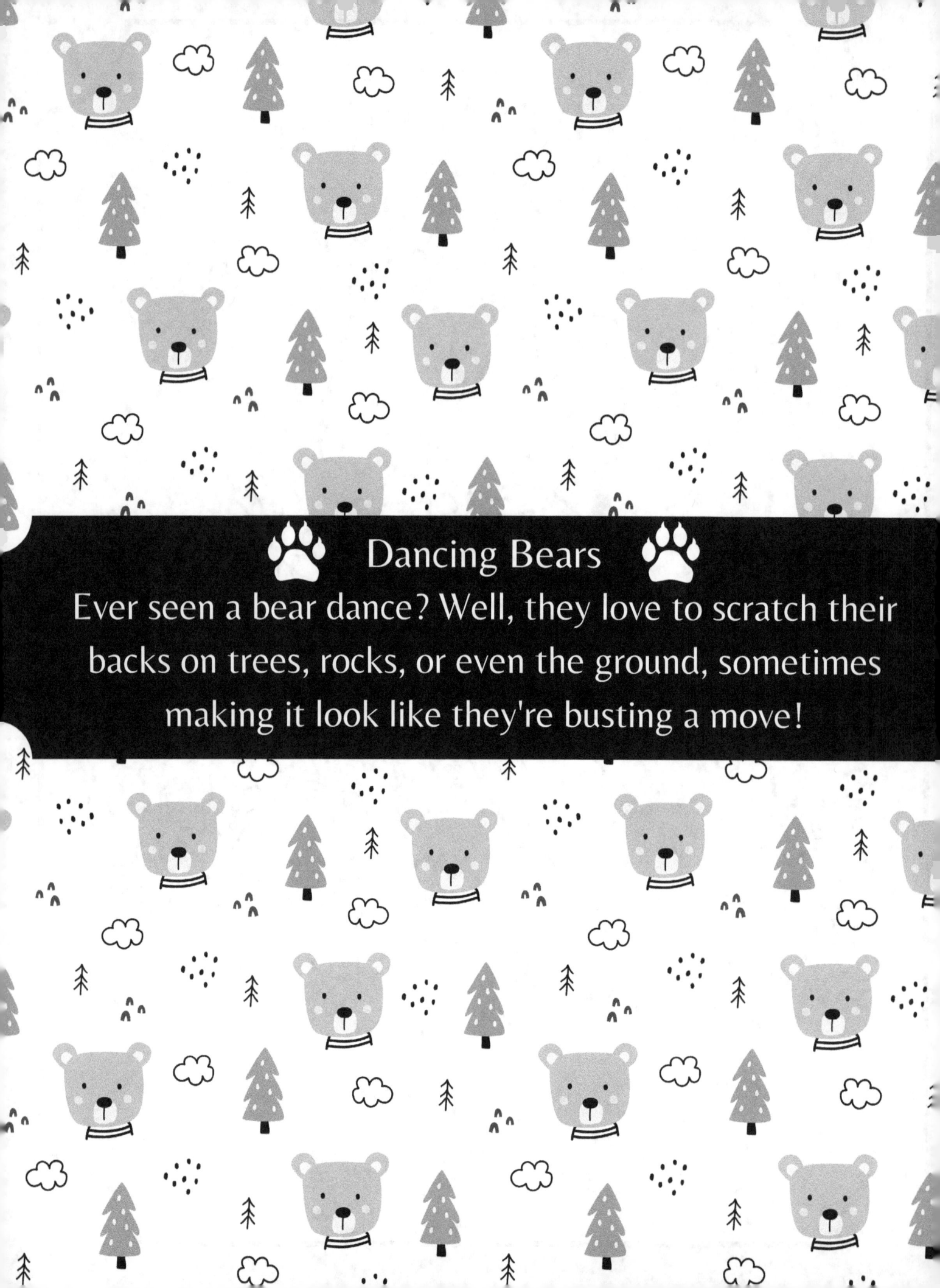

Dancing Bears

Ever seen a bear dance? Well, they love to scratch their backs on trees, rocks, or even the ground, sometimes making it look like they're busting a move!

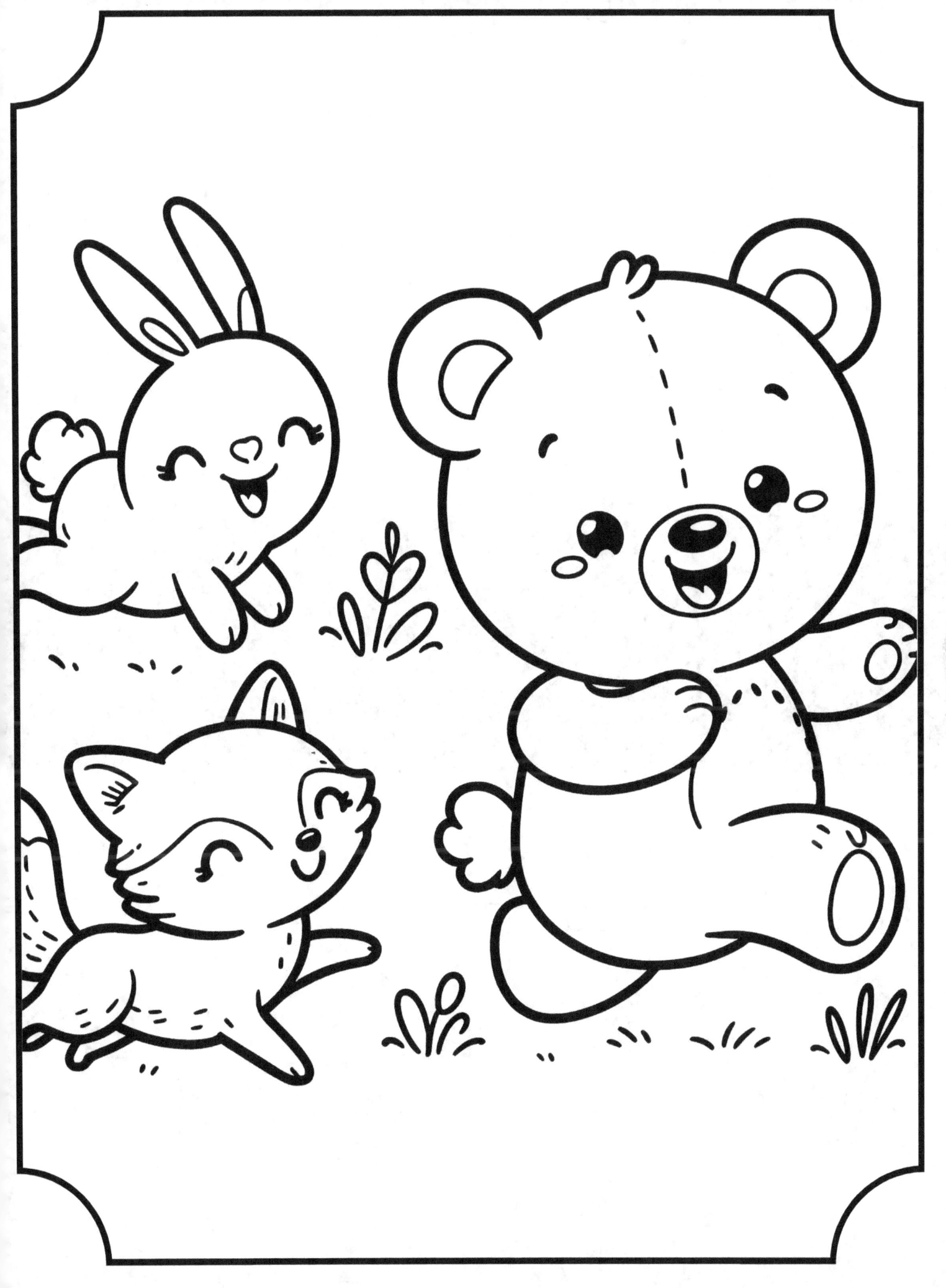

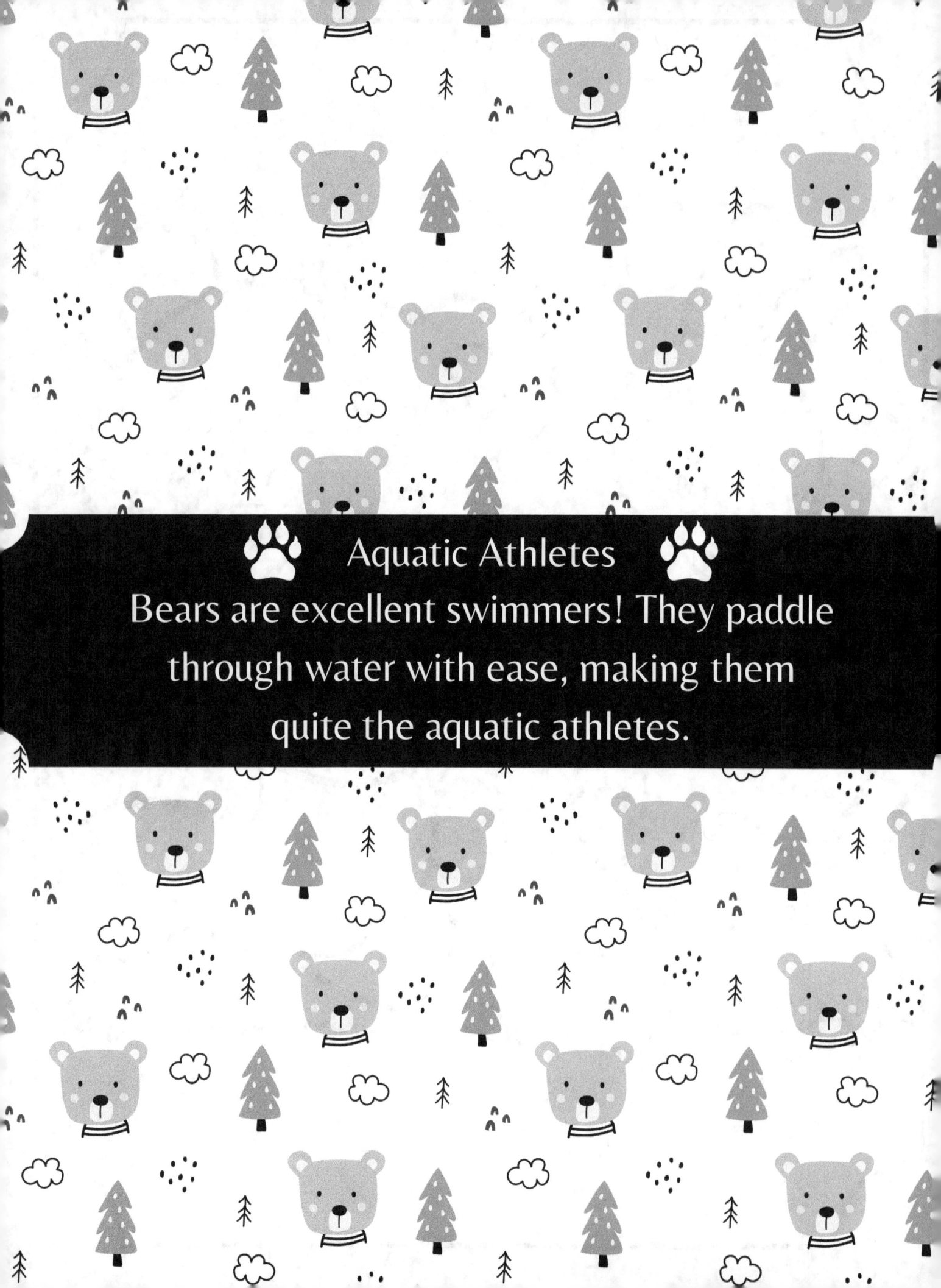

🐾 Aquatic Athletes 🐾
Bears are excellent swimmers! They paddle through water with ease, making them quite the aquatic athletes.

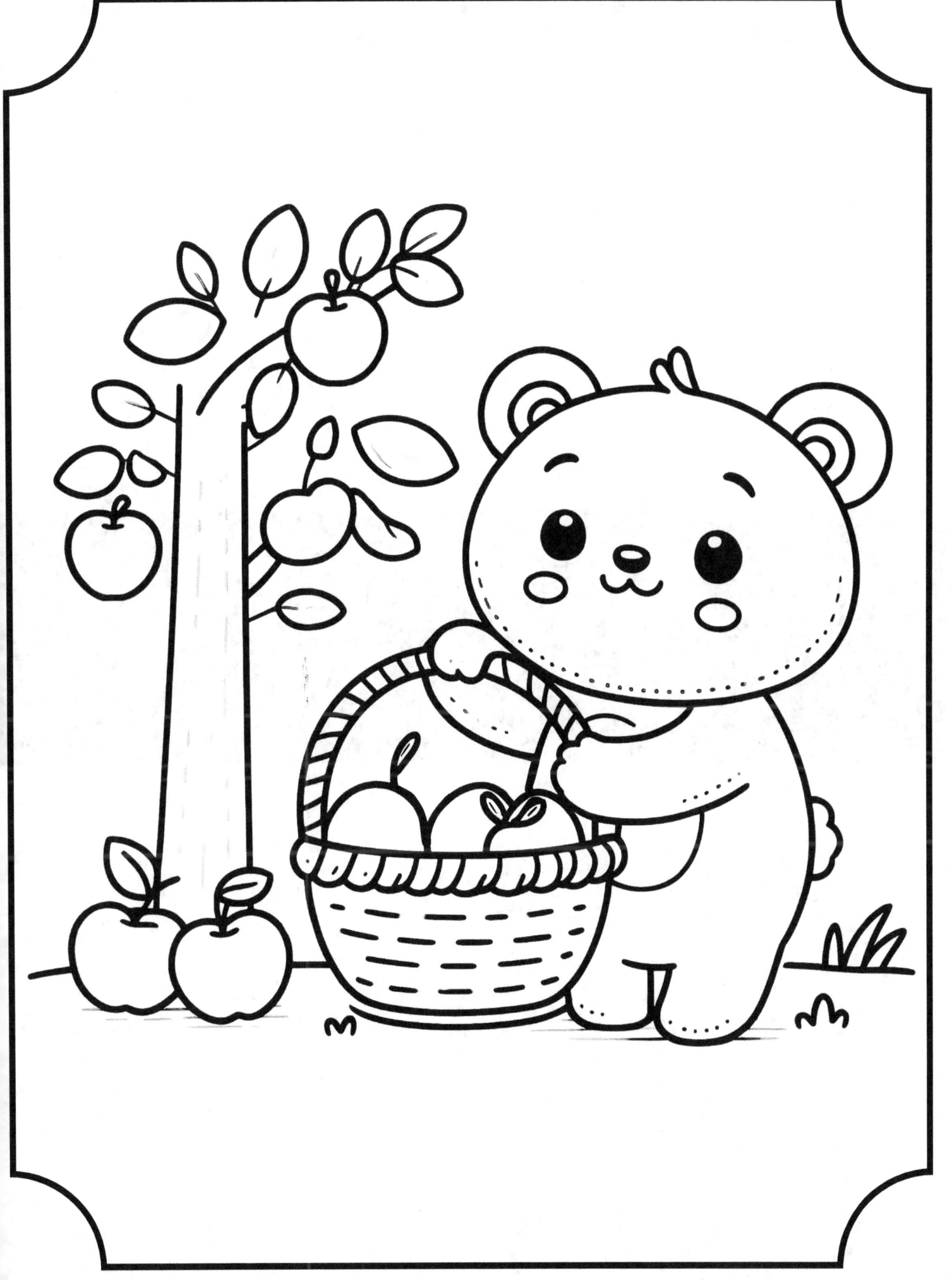

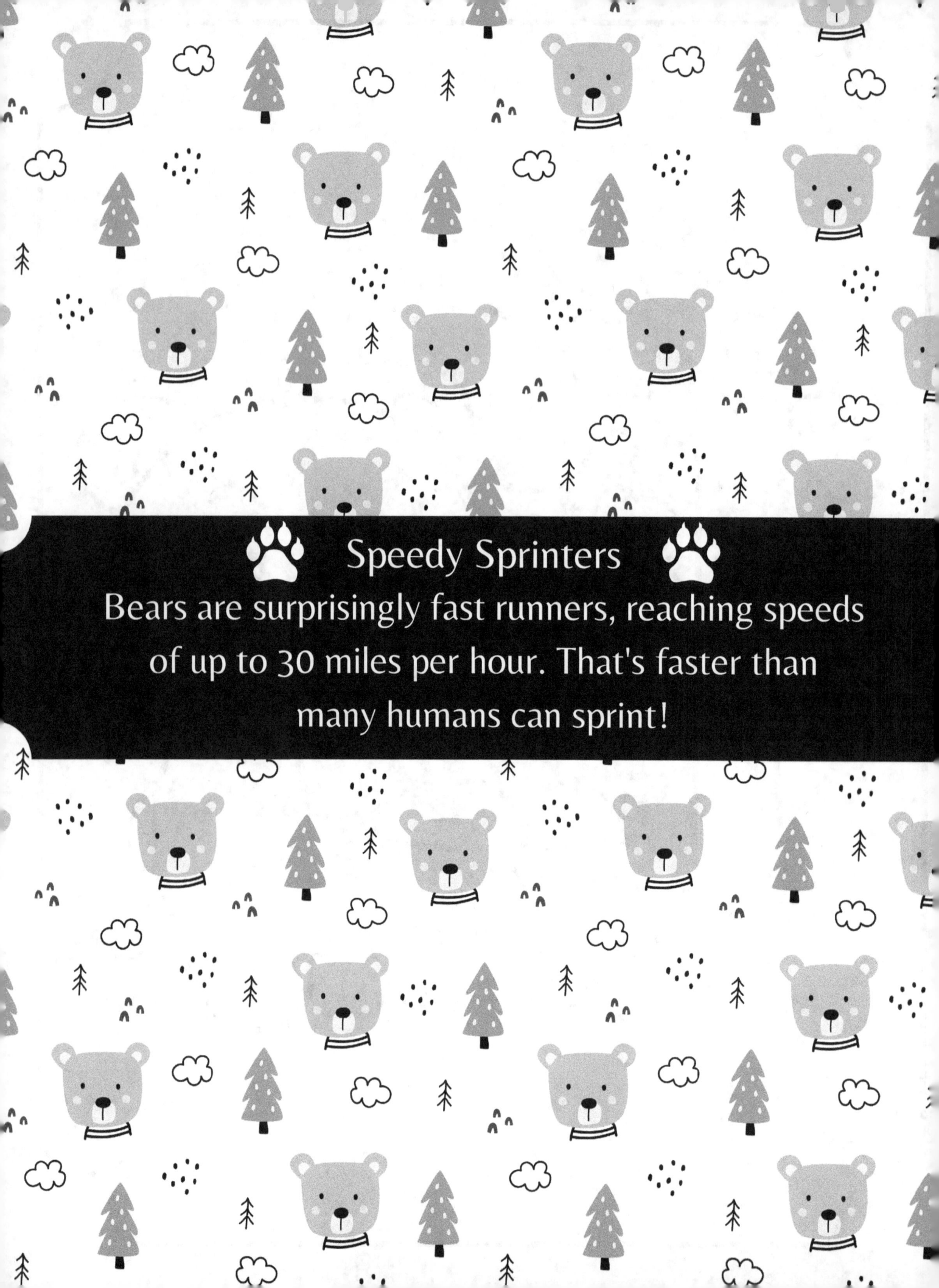

Speedy Sprinters
Bears are surprisingly fast runners, reaching speeds of up to 30 miles per hour. That's faster than many humans can sprint!

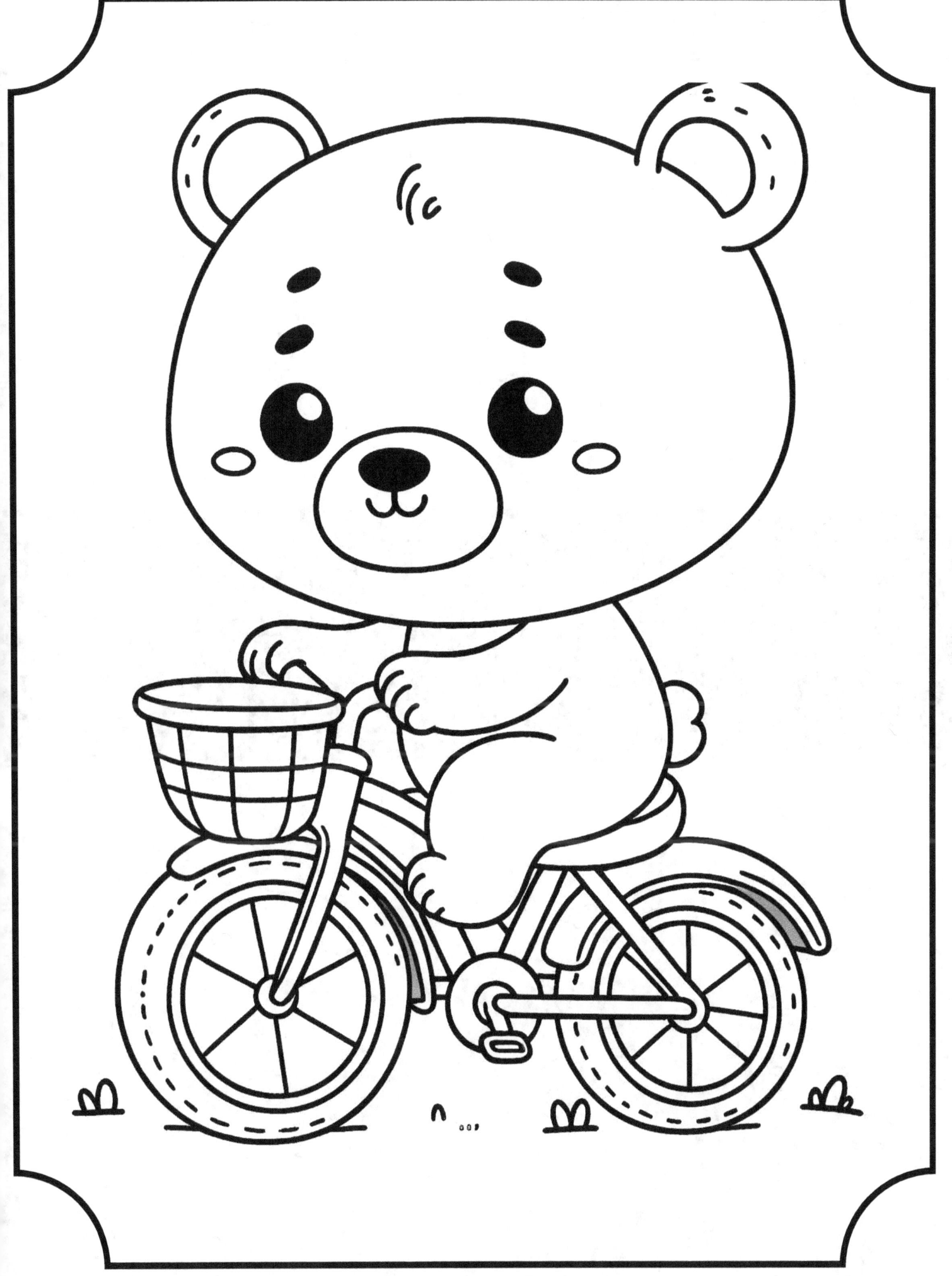

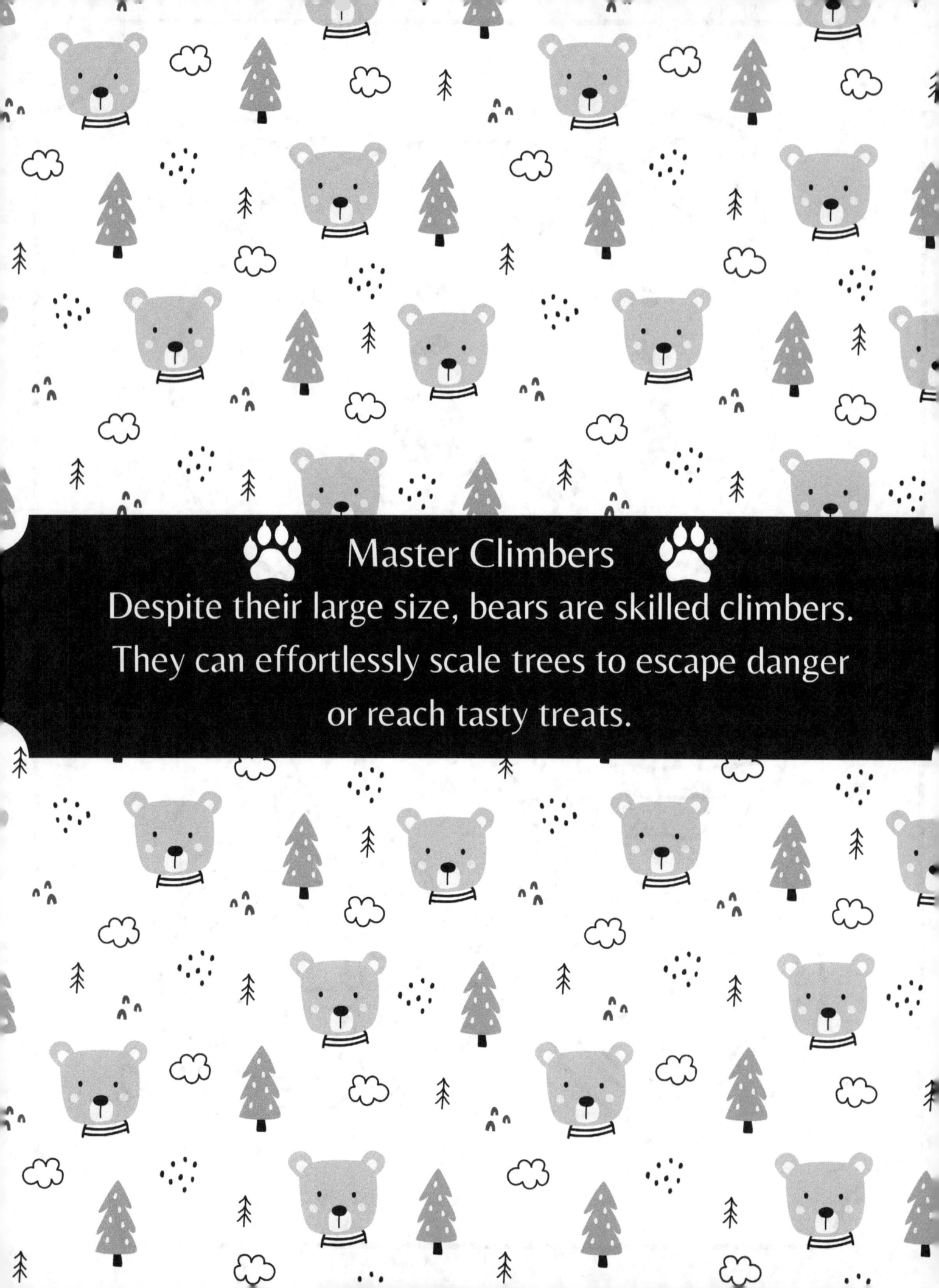

Master Climbers
Despite their large size, bears are skilled climbers. They can effortlessly scale trees to escape danger or reach tasty treats.

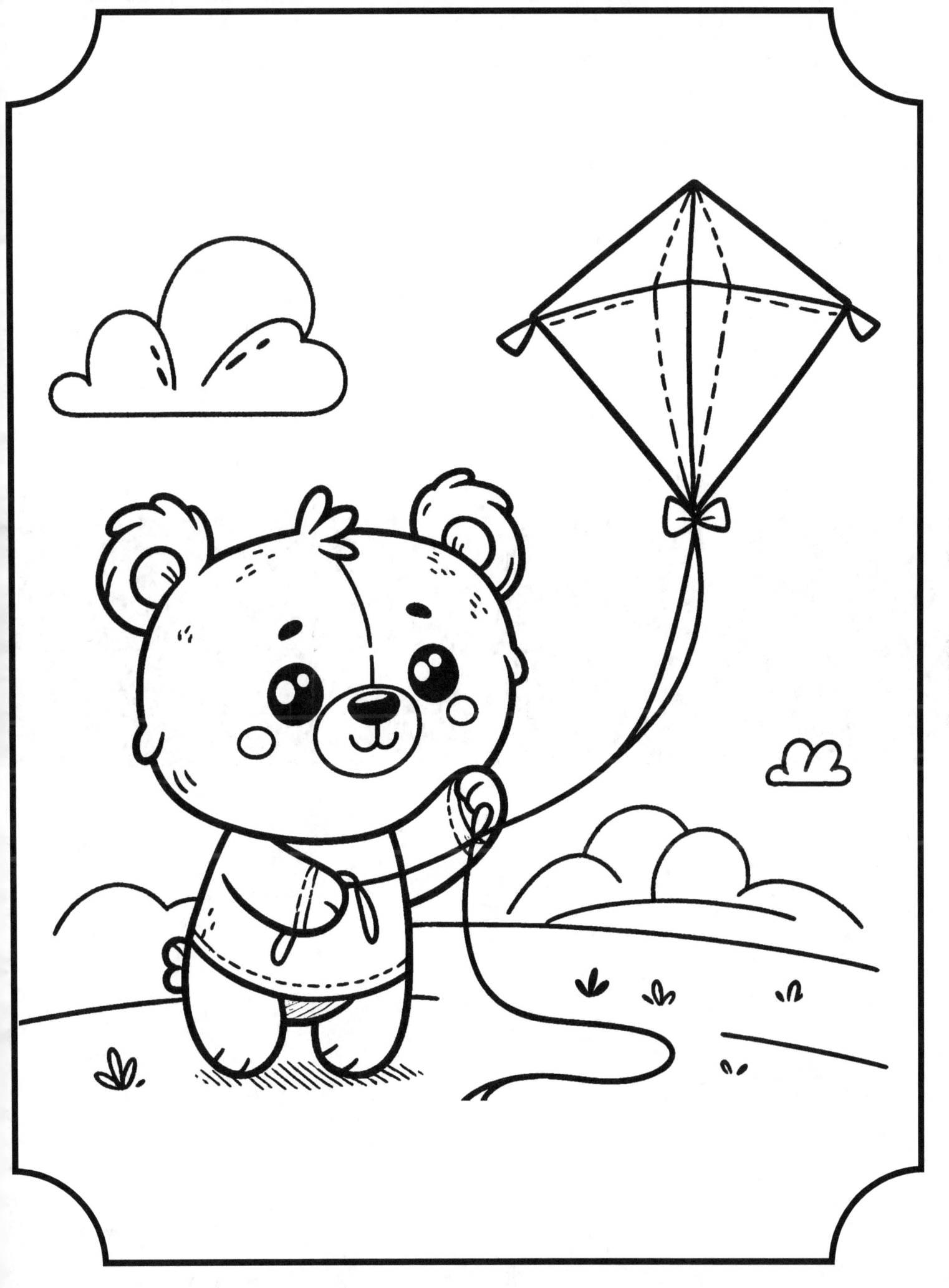

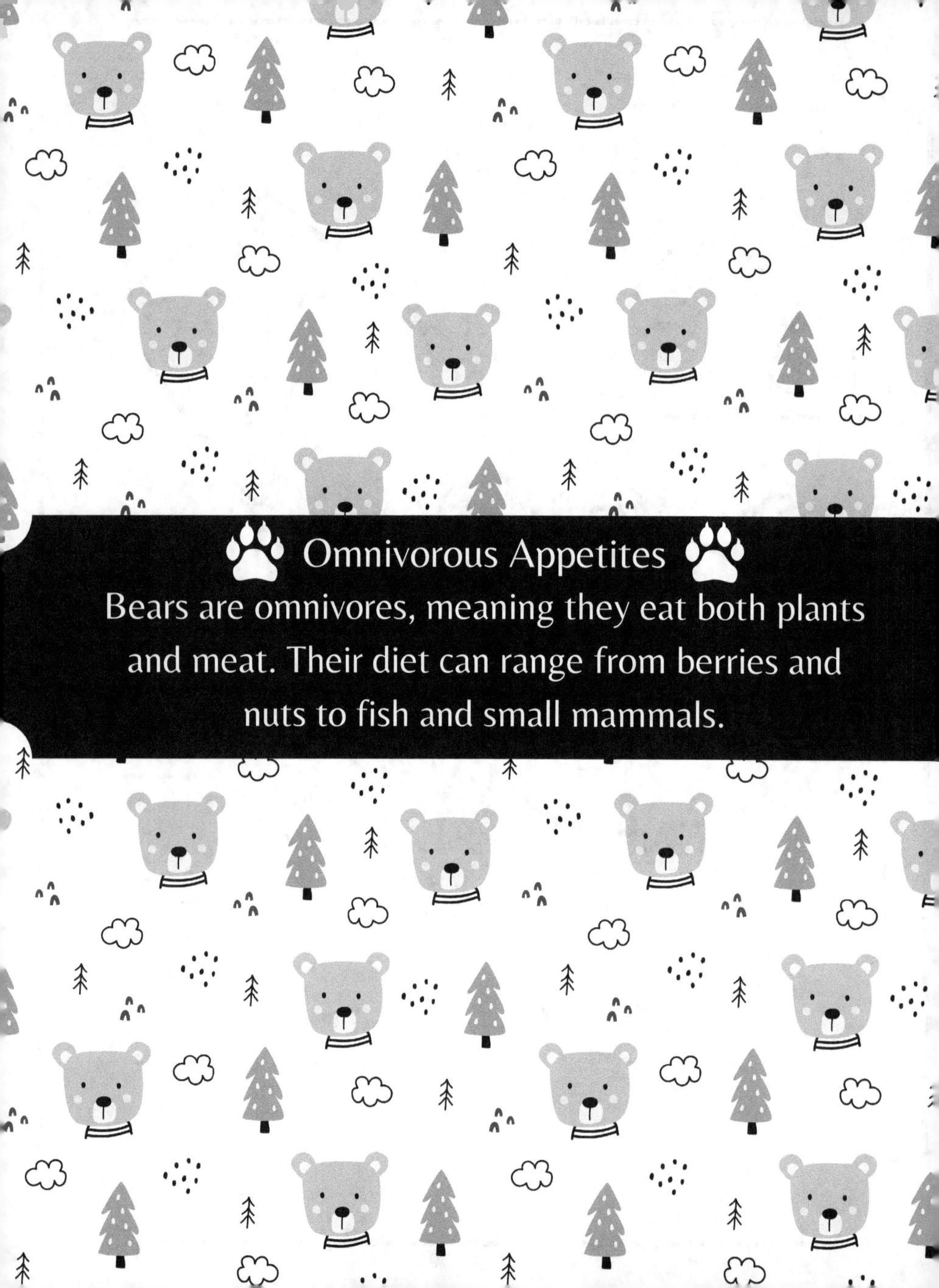

🐾 Omnivorous Appetites 🐾
Bears are omnivores, meaning they eat both plants and meat. Their diet can range from berries and nuts to fish and small mammals.

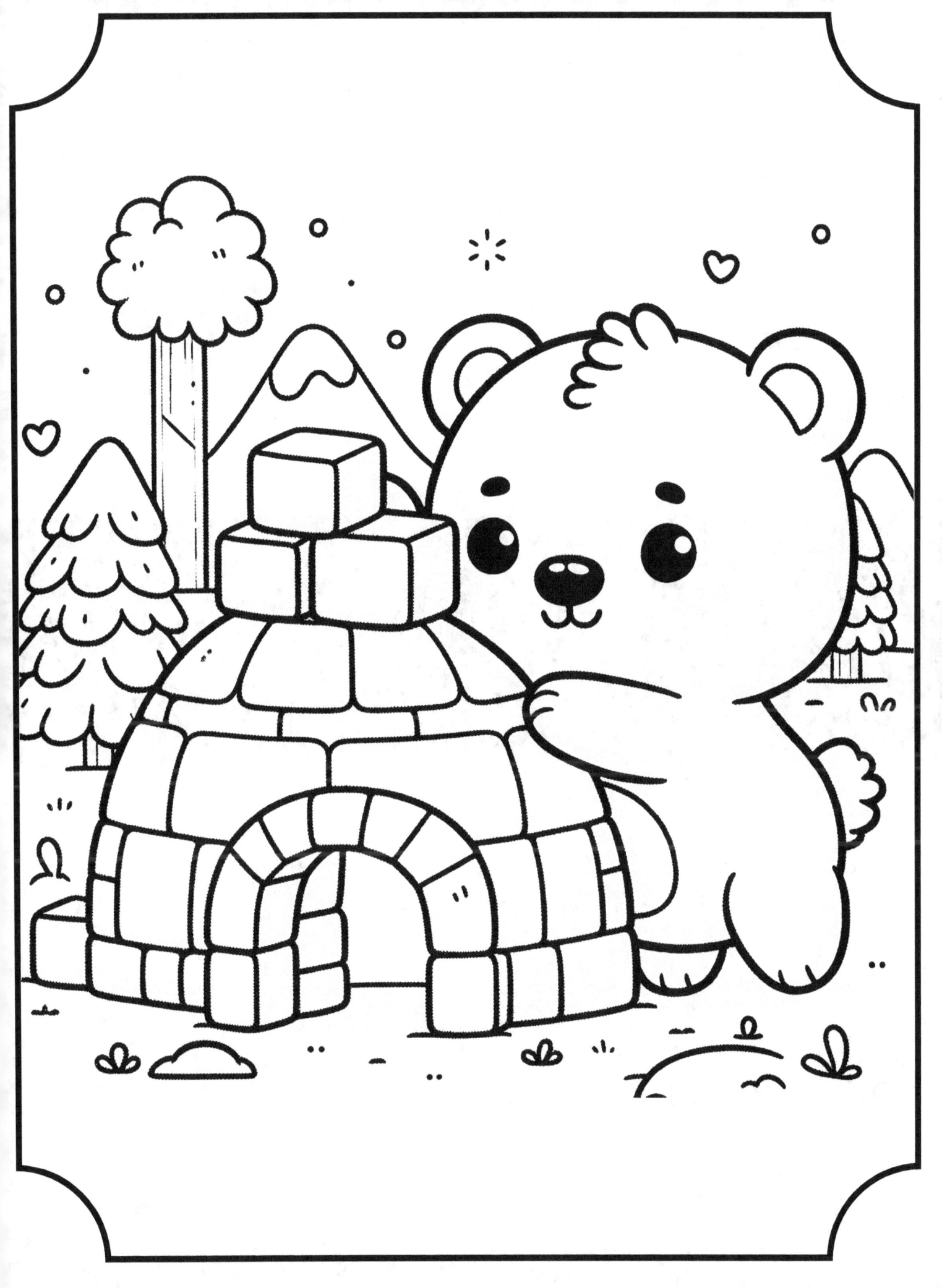

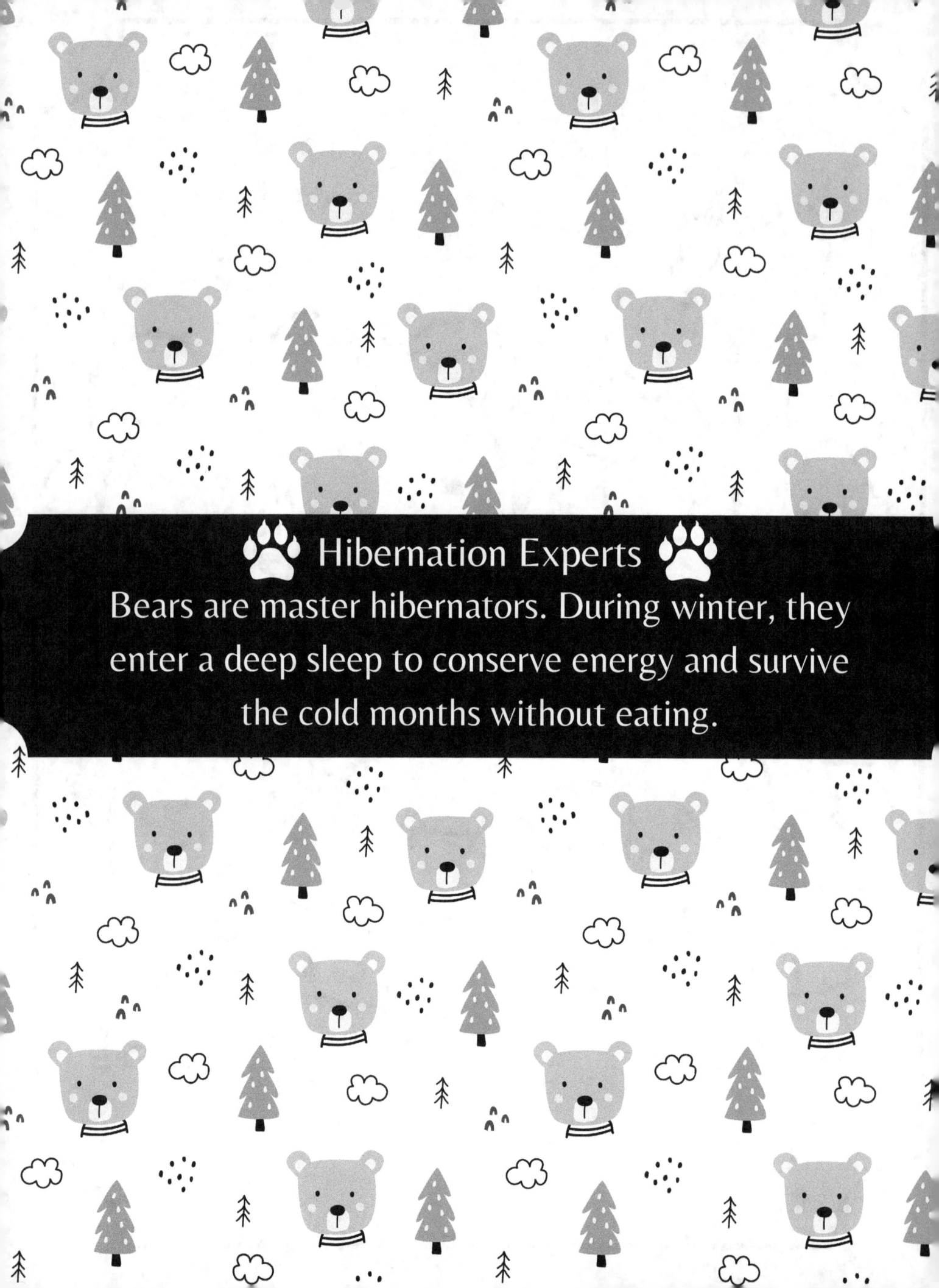

🐾 Hibernation Experts 🐾
Bears are master hibernators. During winter, they enter a deep sleep to conserve energy and survive the cold months without eating.

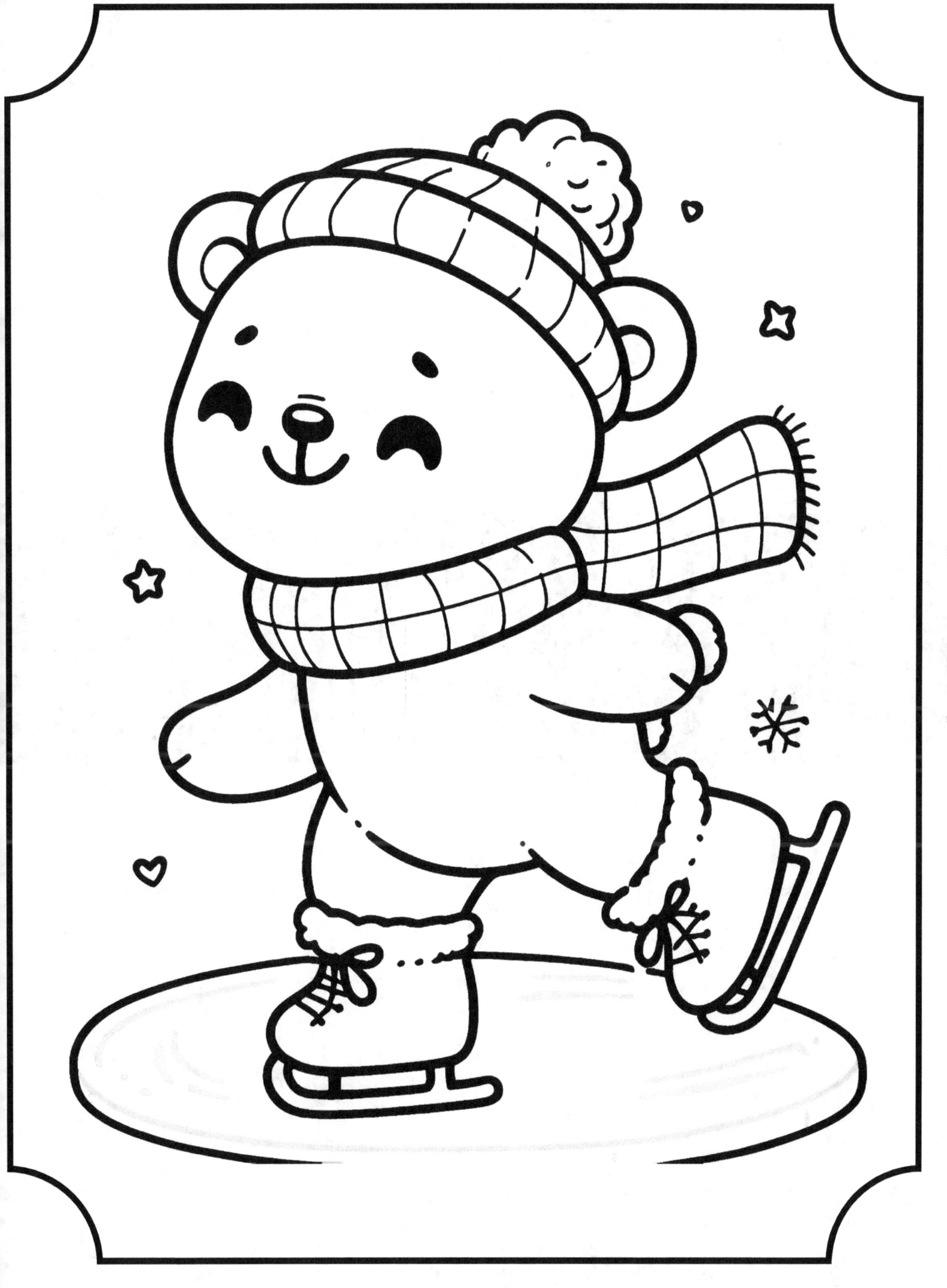

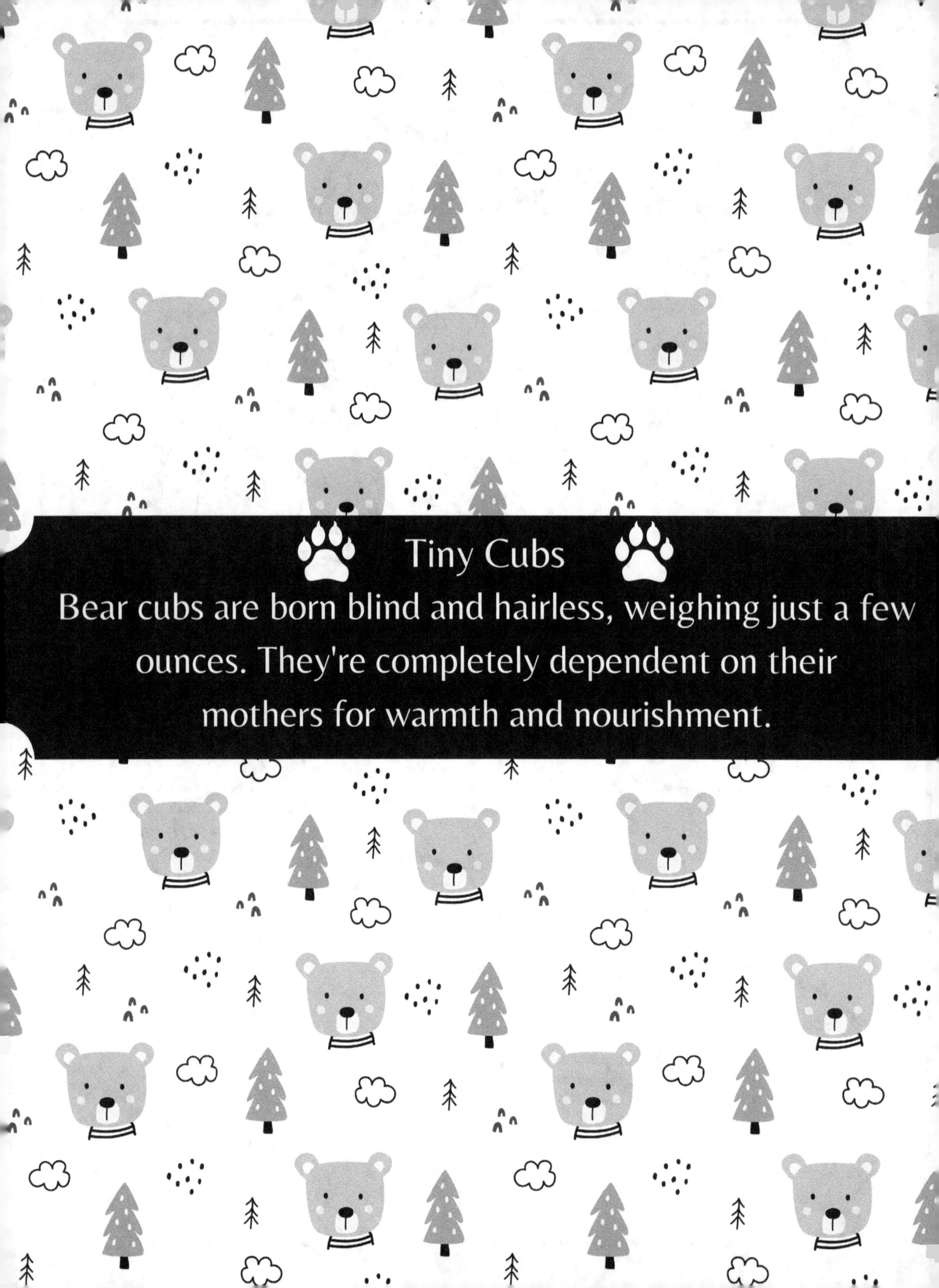

Tiny Cubs

Bear cubs are born blind and hairless, weighing just a few ounces. They're completely dependent on their mothers for warmth and nourishment.

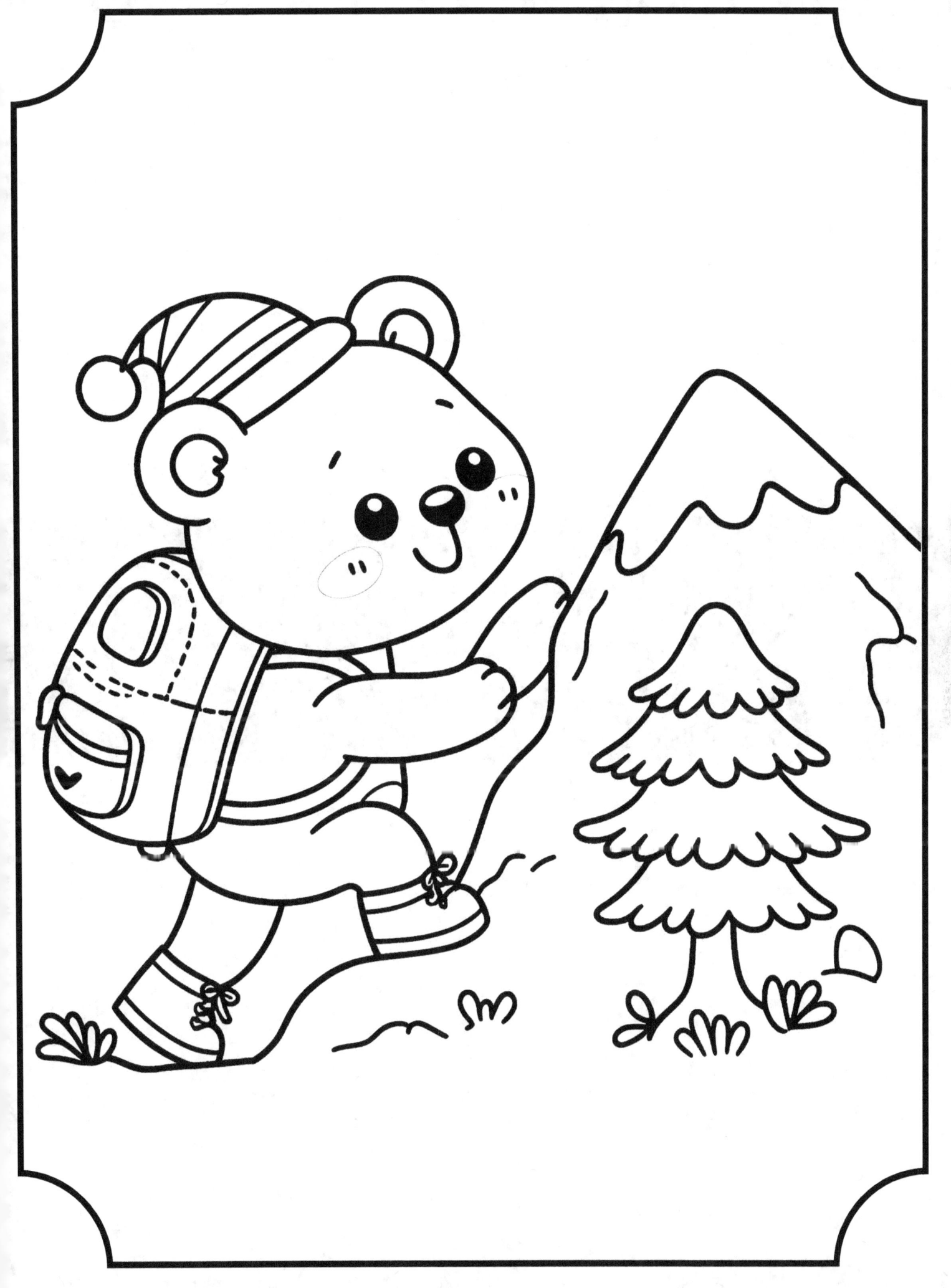

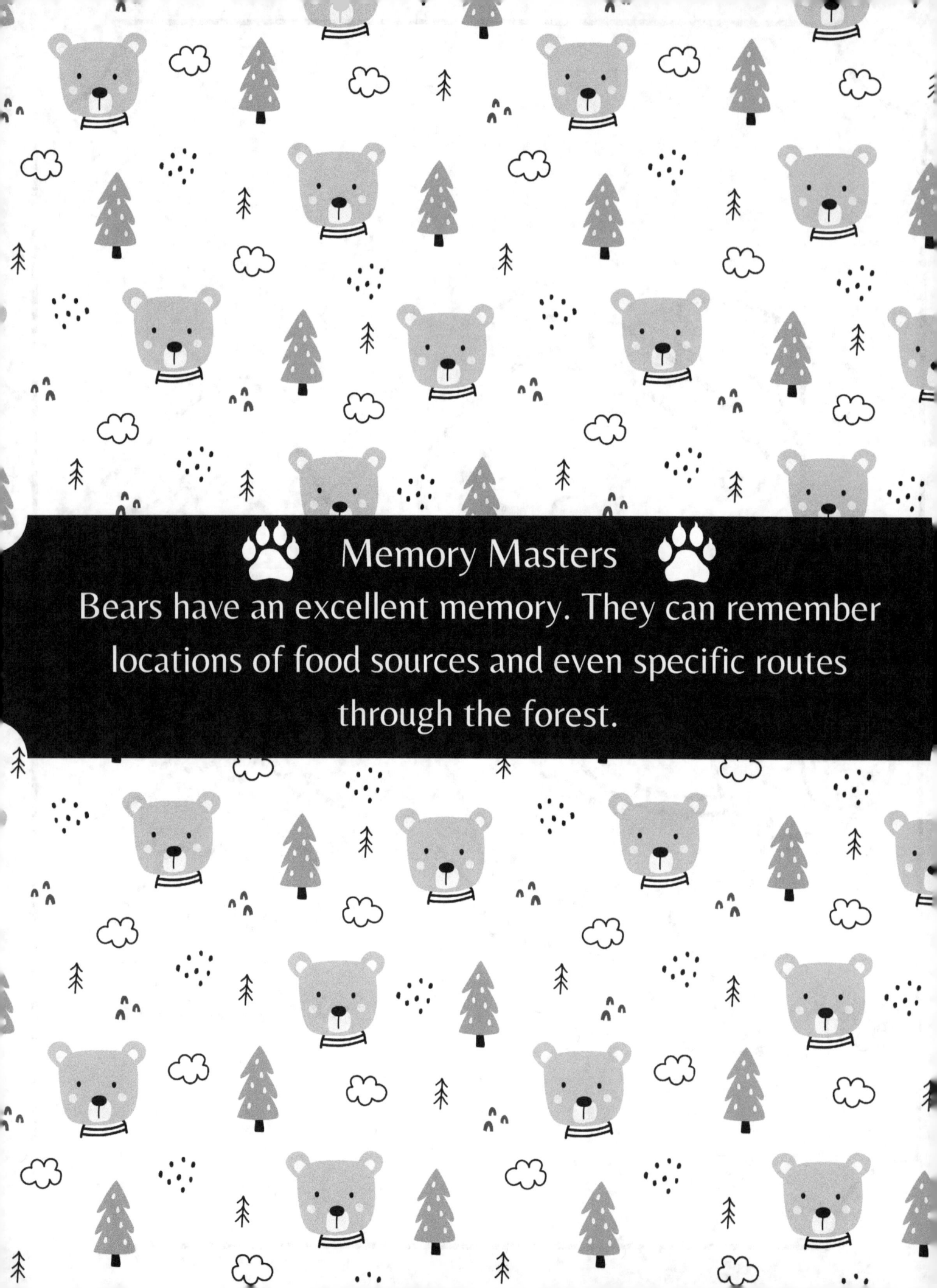

Memory Masters
Bears have an excellent memory. They can remember locations of food sources and even specific routes through the forest.

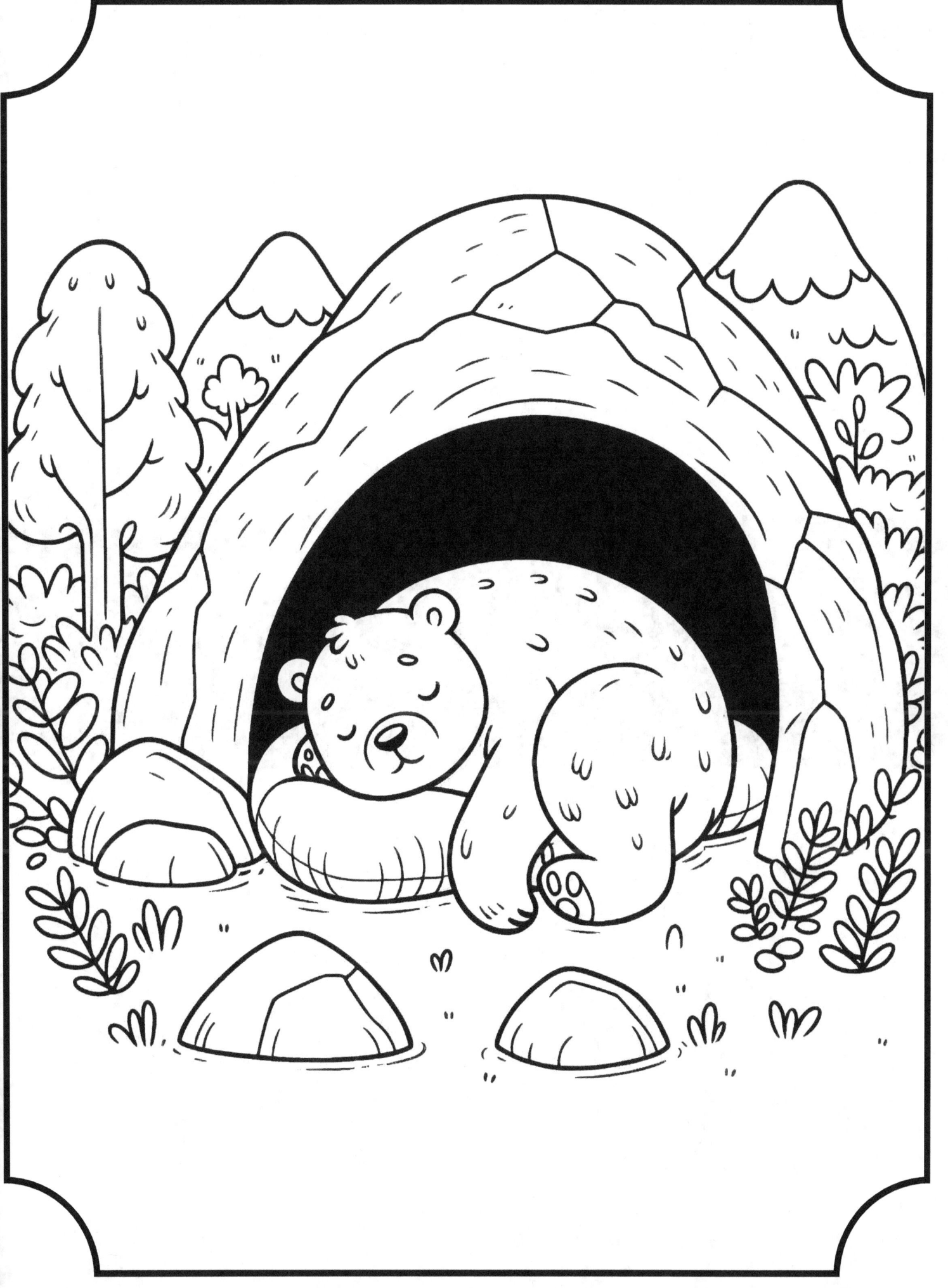

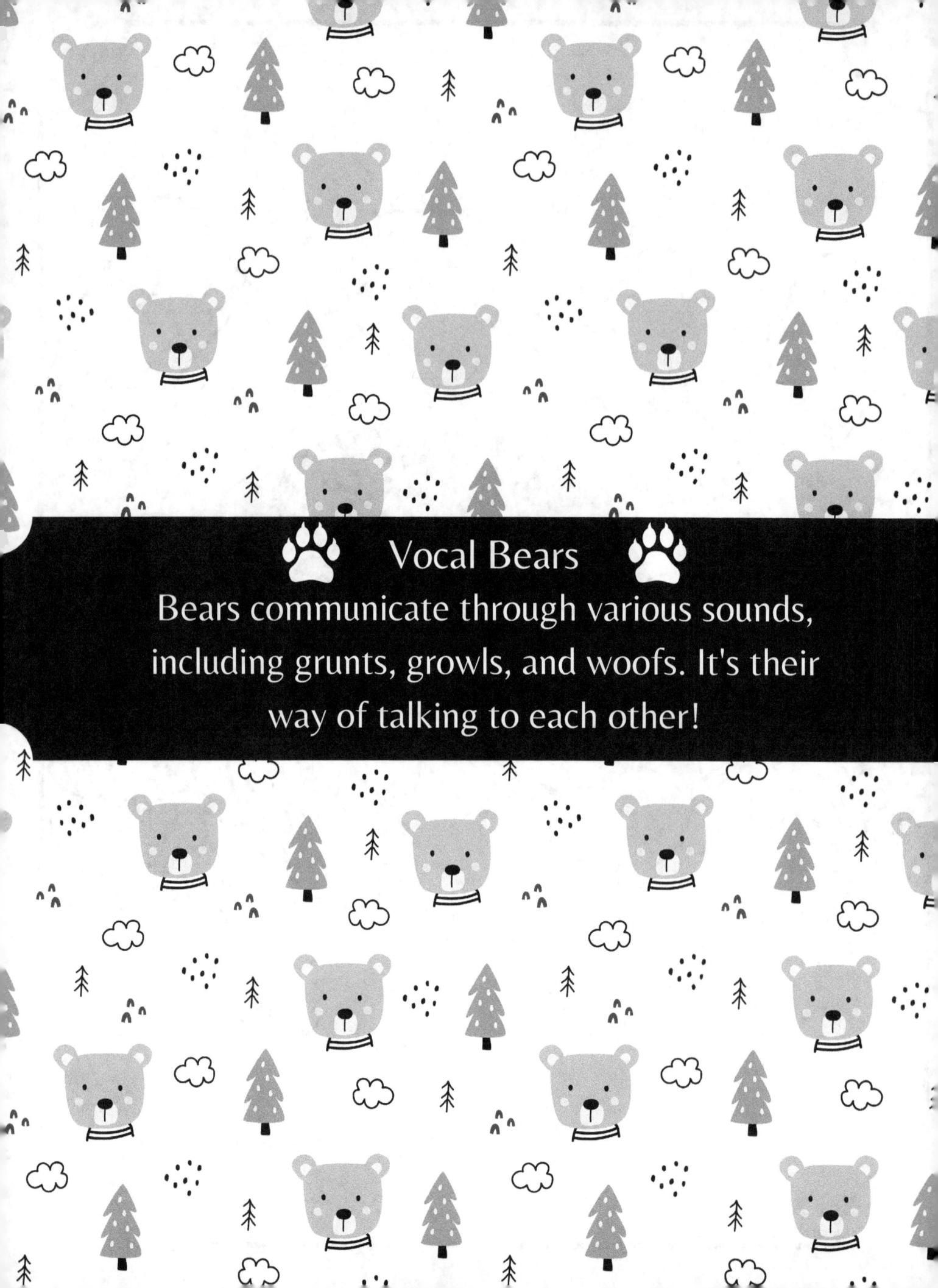

🐾 Vocal Bears 🐾
Bears communicate through various sounds, including grunts, growls, and woofs. It's their way of talking to each other!

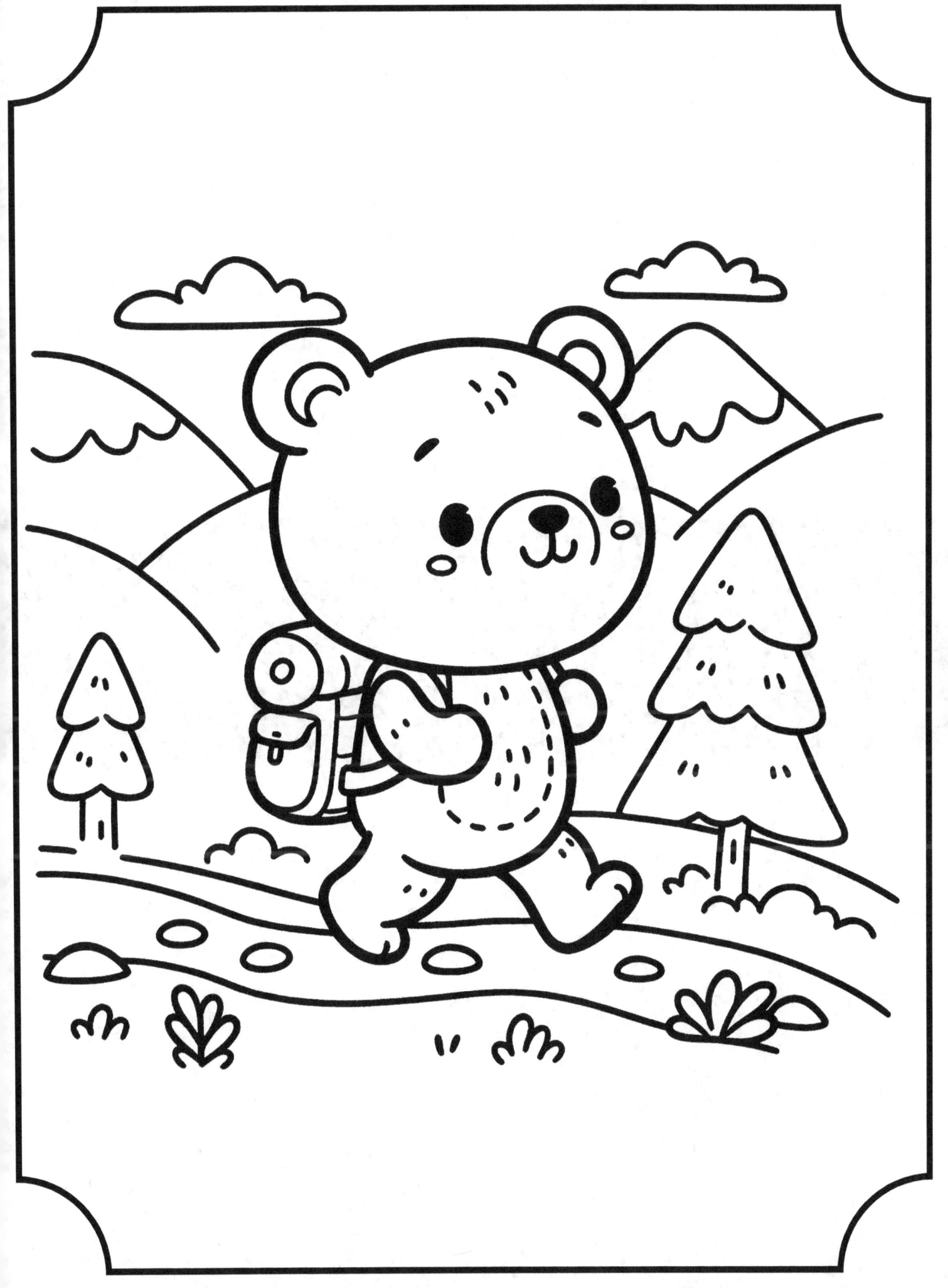

Territorial Markers

Bears have a unique way of marking their territory, they leave behind scent markings on trees or rocks by rubbing against them.

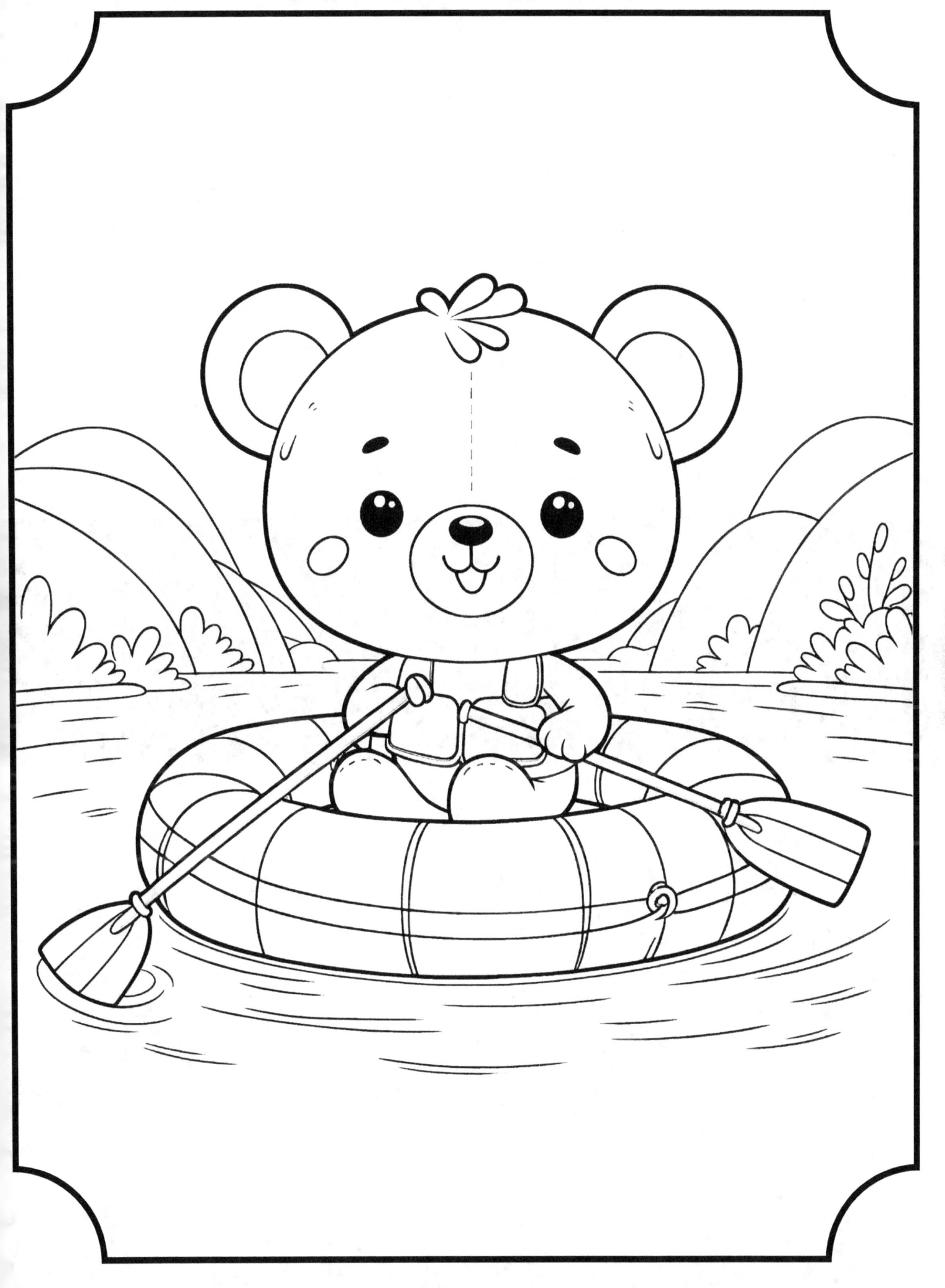

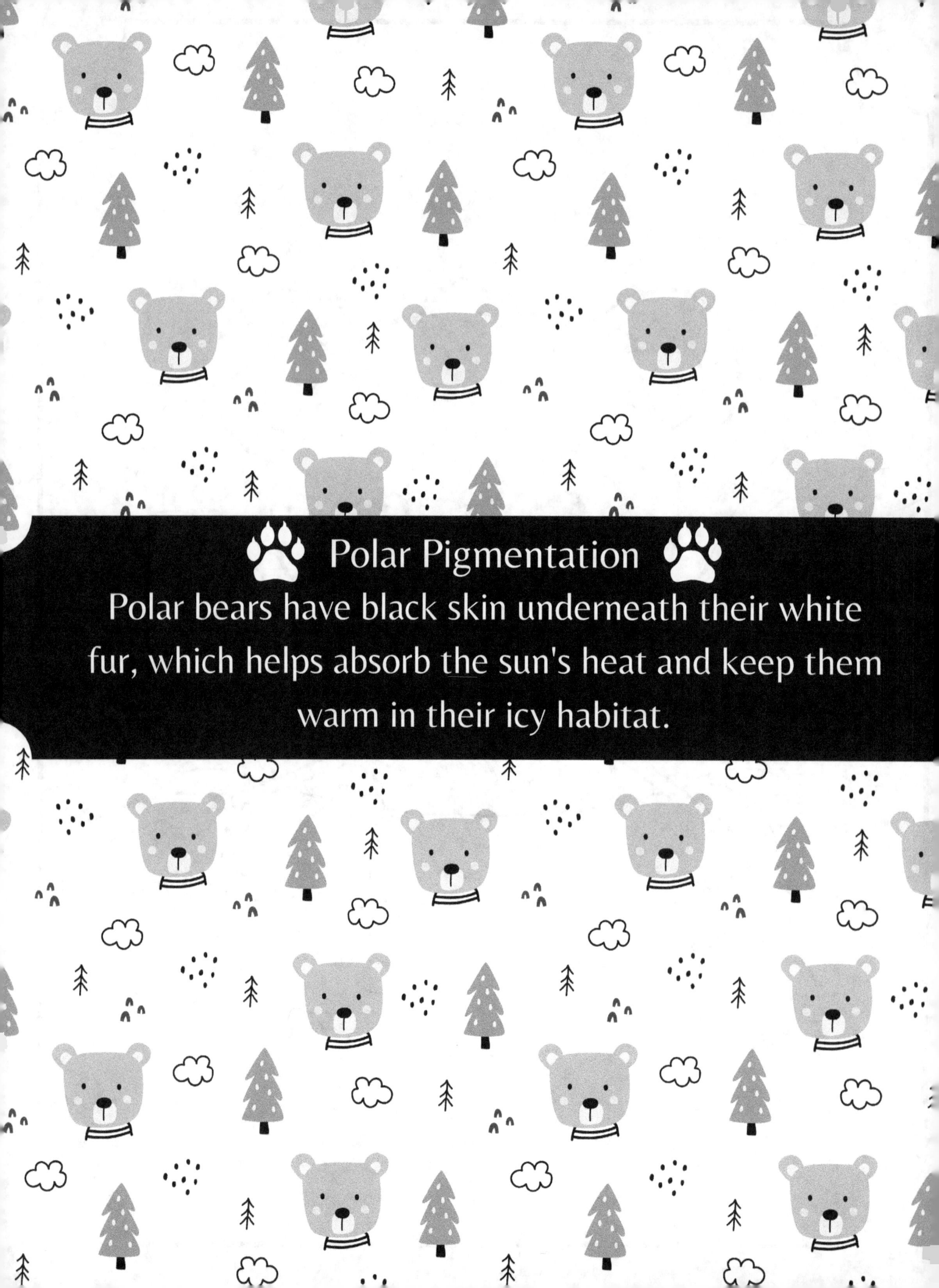

🐾 Polar Pigmentation 🐾
Polar bears have black skin underneath their white fur, which helps absorb the sun's heat and keep them warm in their icy habitat.

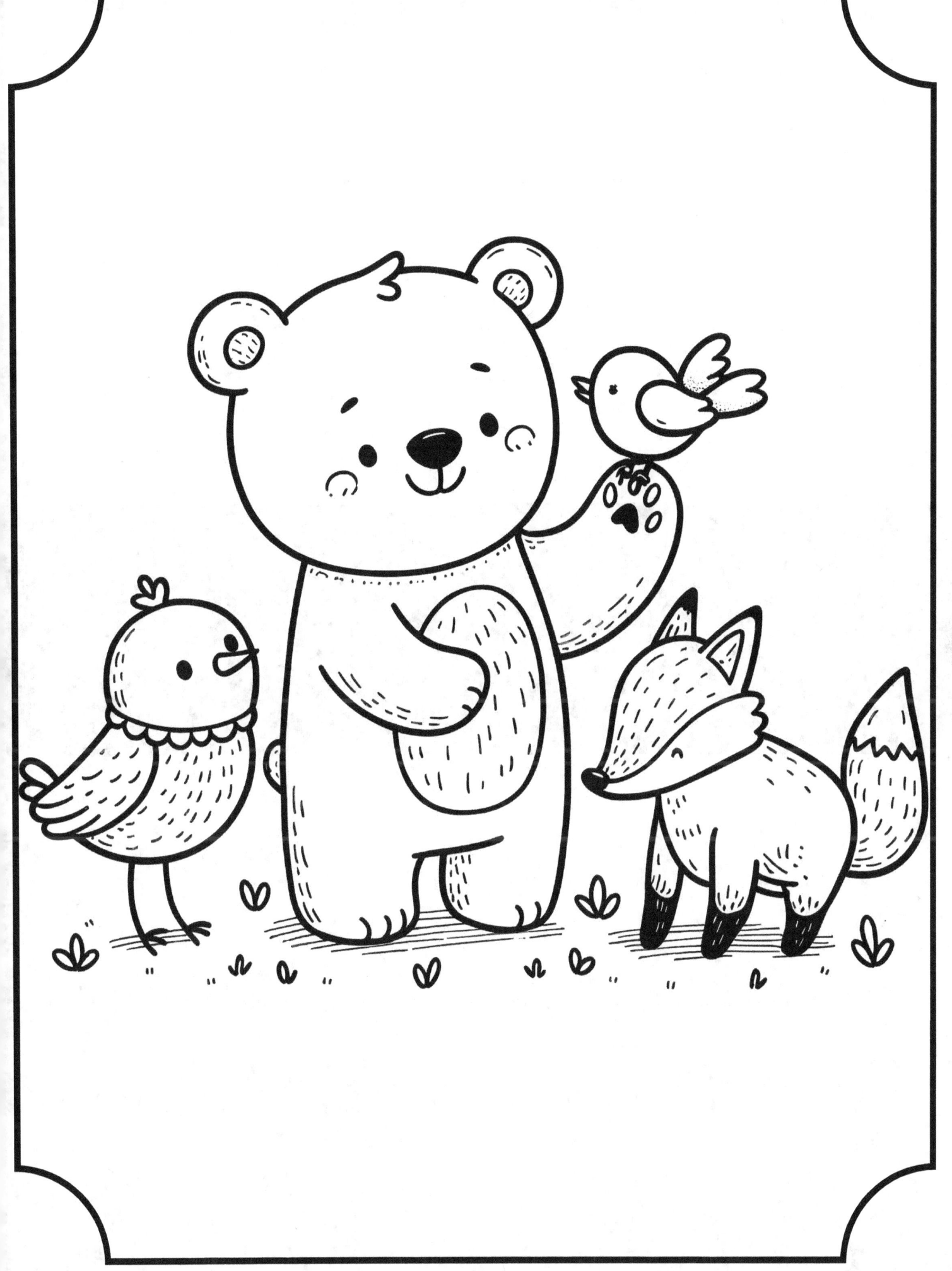

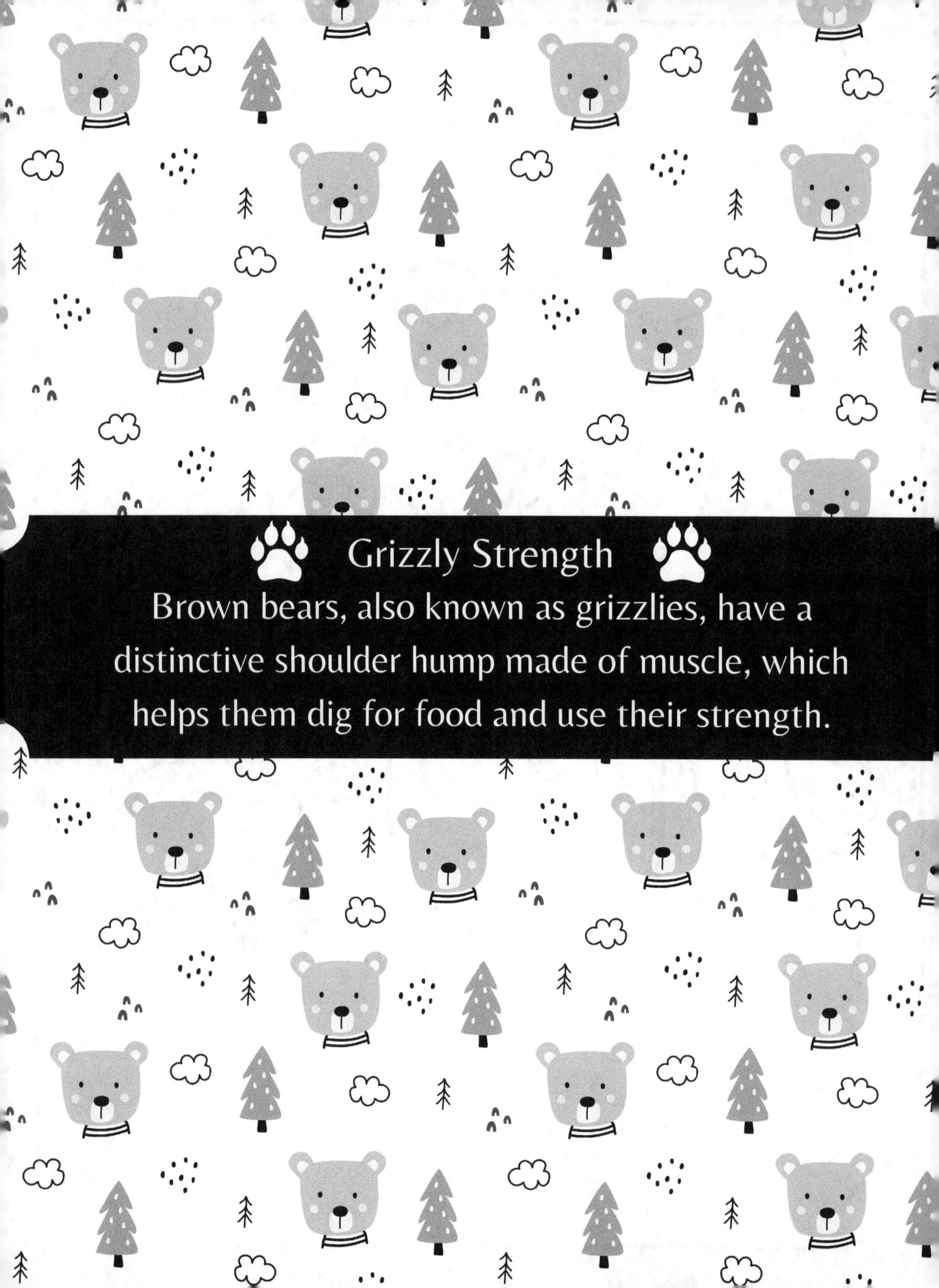

Grizzly Strength

Brown bears, also known as grizzlies, have a distinctive shoulder hump made of muscle, which helps them dig for food and use their strength.

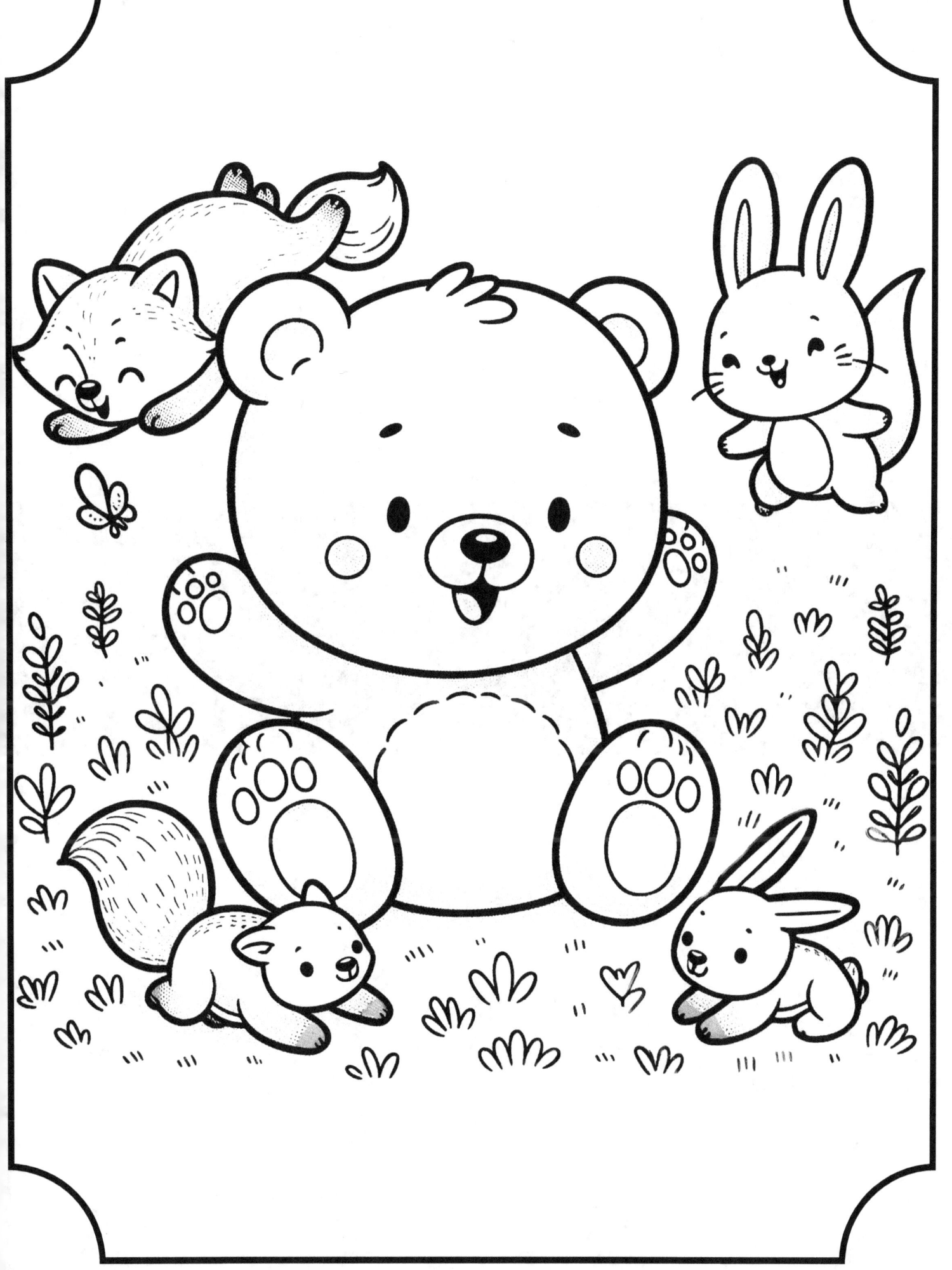

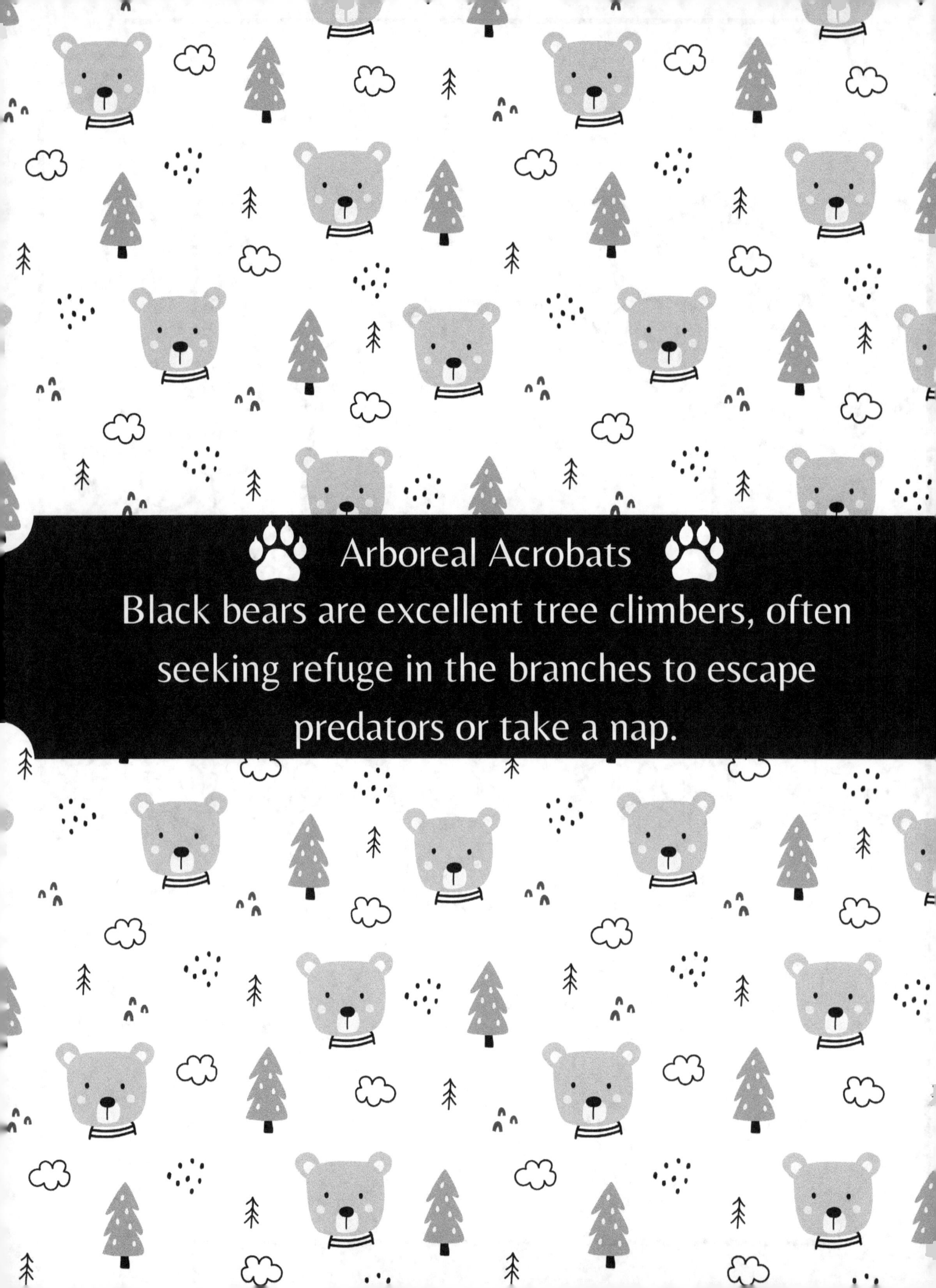

Arboreal Acrobats

Black bears are excellent tree climbers, often seeking refuge in the branches to escape predators or take a nap.

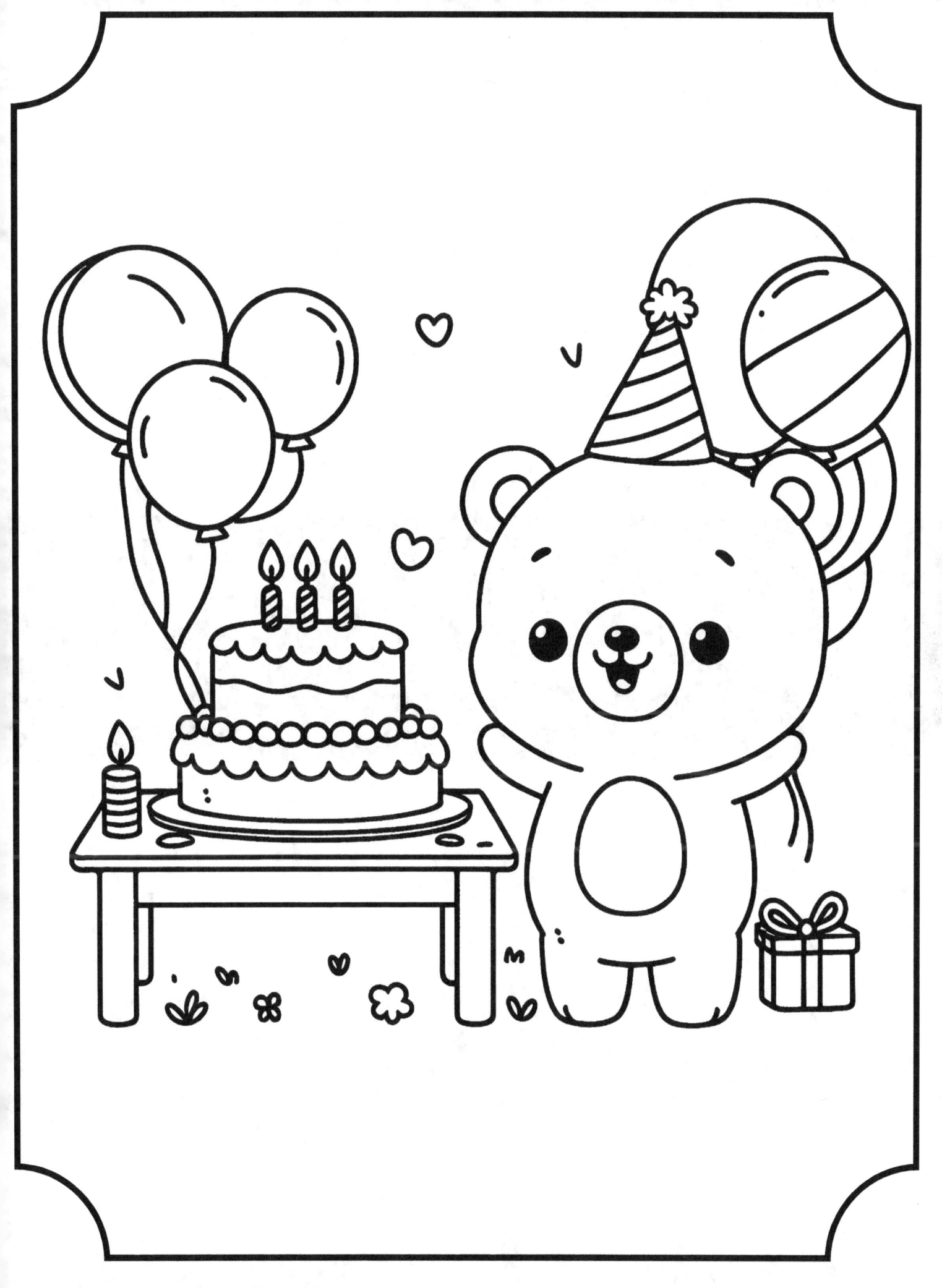

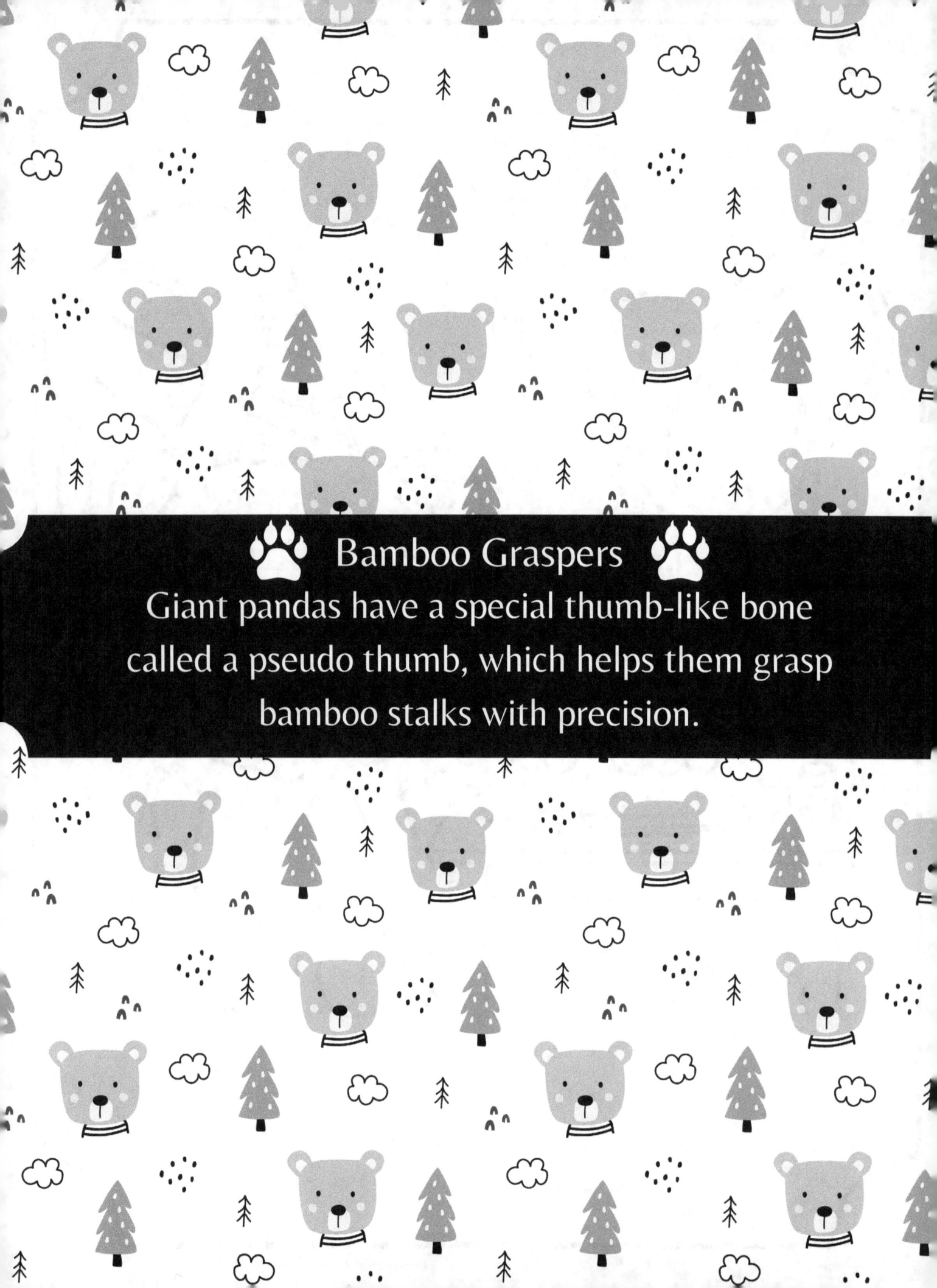

🐾 Bamboo Graspers 🐾
Giant pandas have a special thumb-like bone called a pseudo thumb, which helps them grasp bamboo stalks with precision.

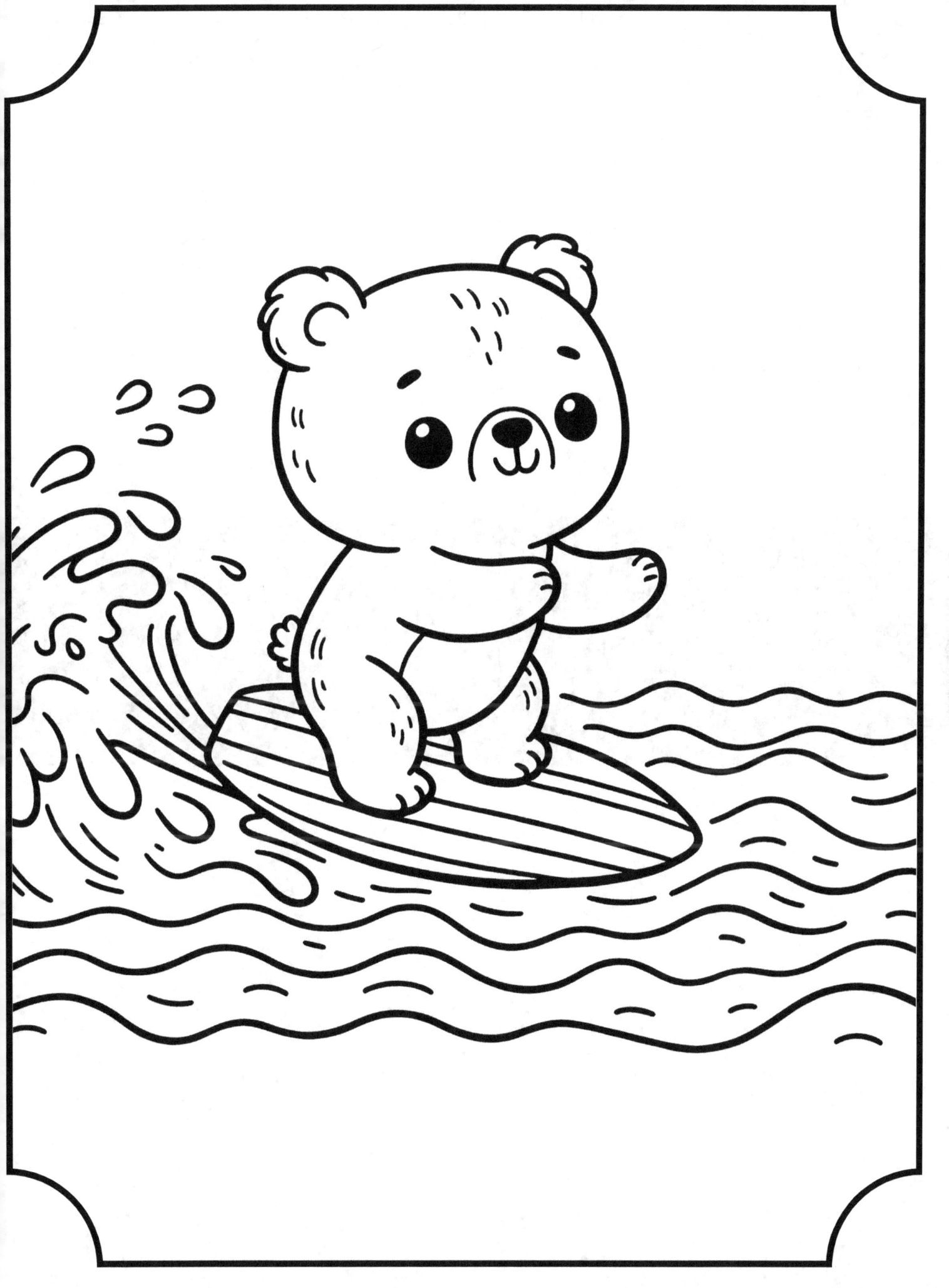

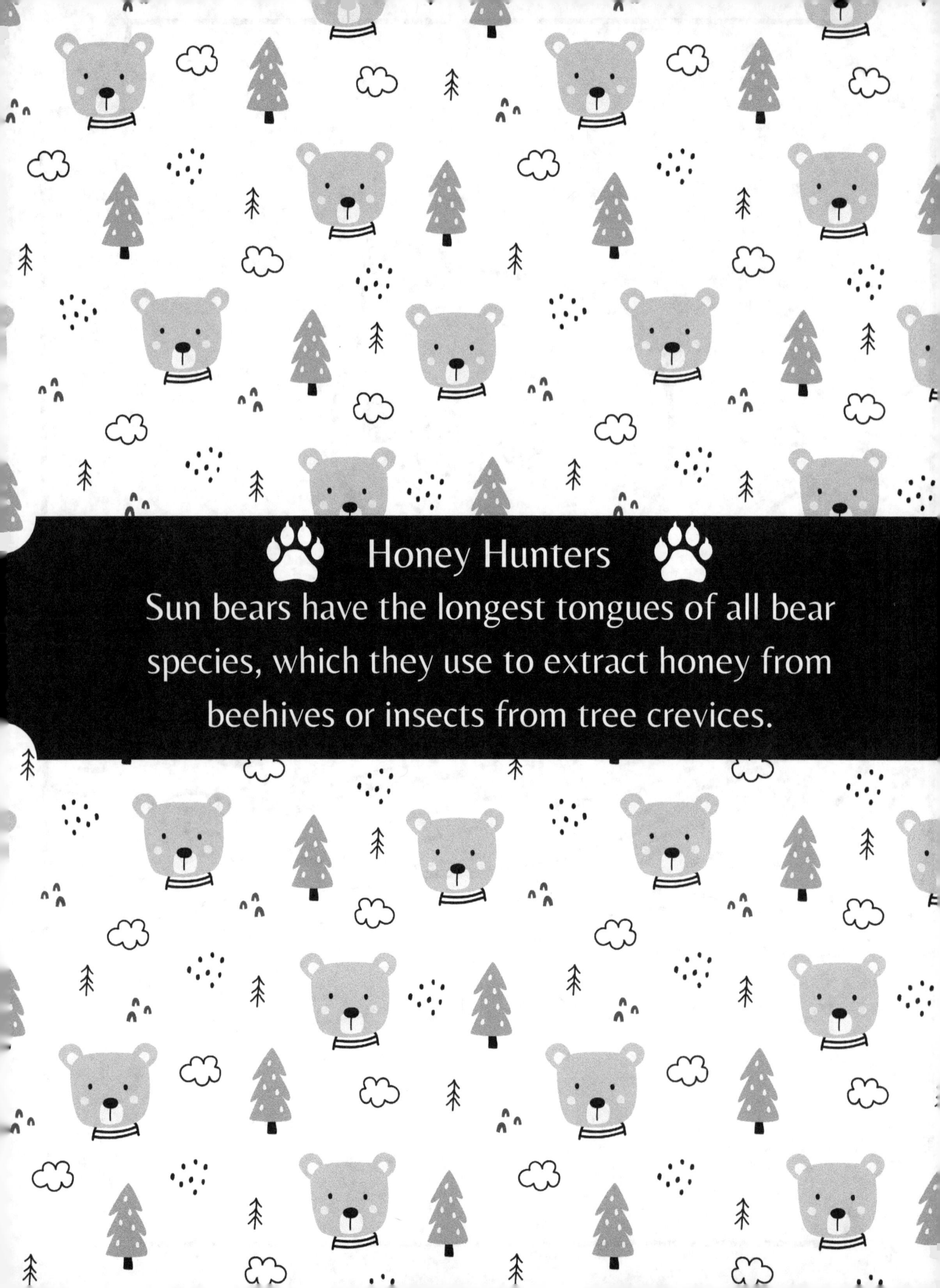

Honey Hunters

Sun bears have the longest tongues of all bear species, which they use to extract honey from beehives or insects from tree crevices.

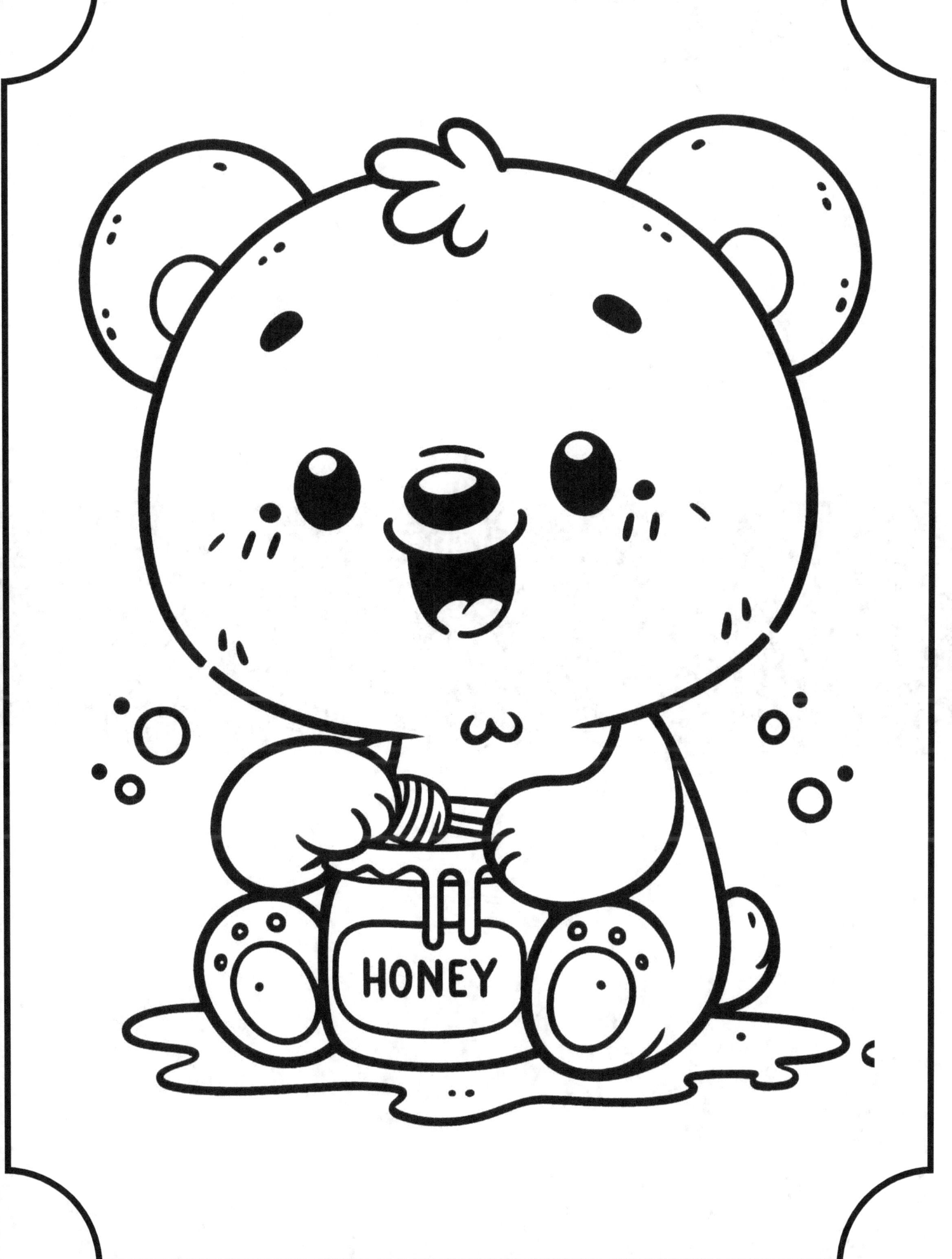

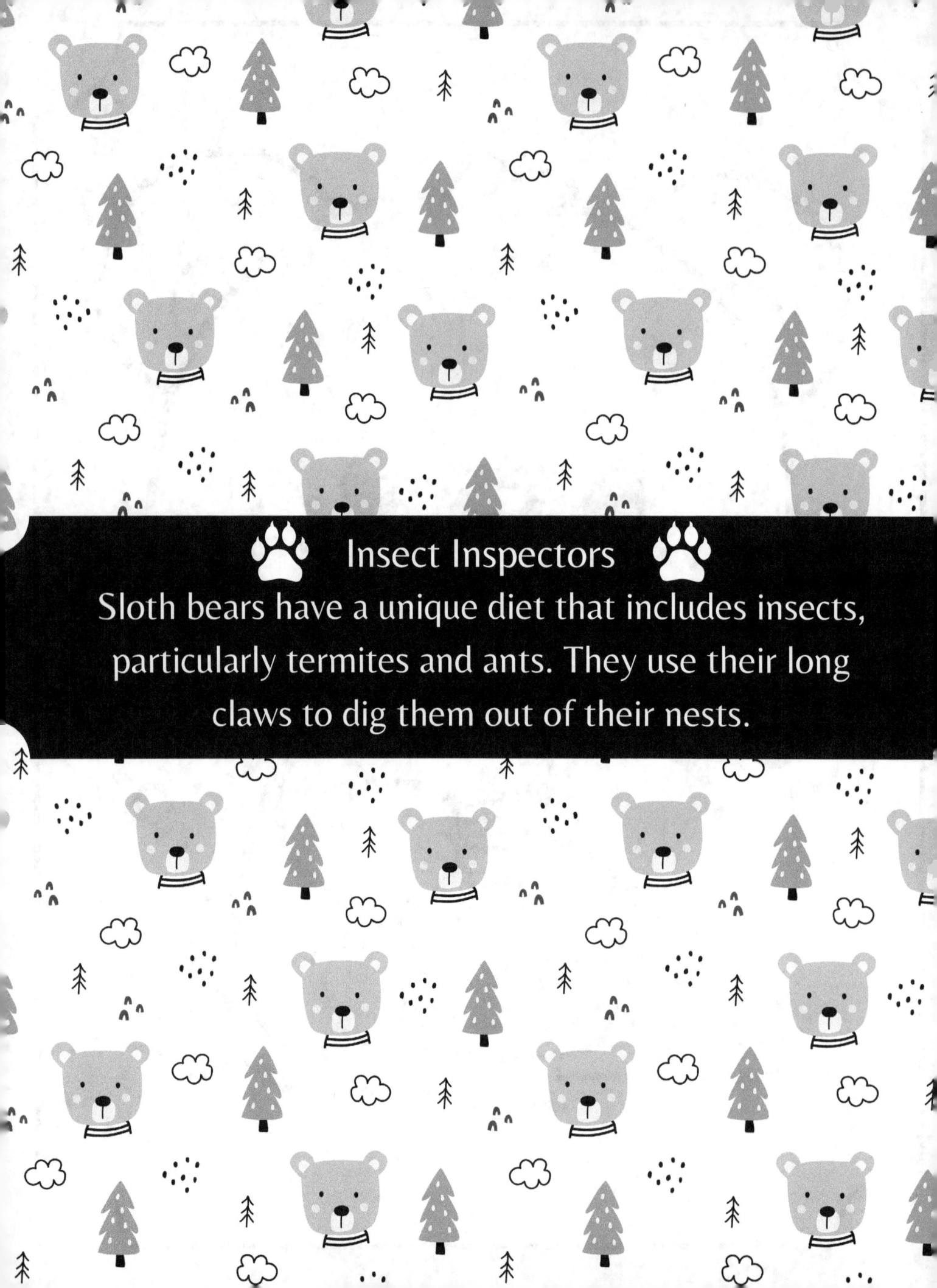

Insect Inspectors

Sloth bears have a unique diet that includes insects, particularly termites and ants. They use their long claws to dig them out of their nests.

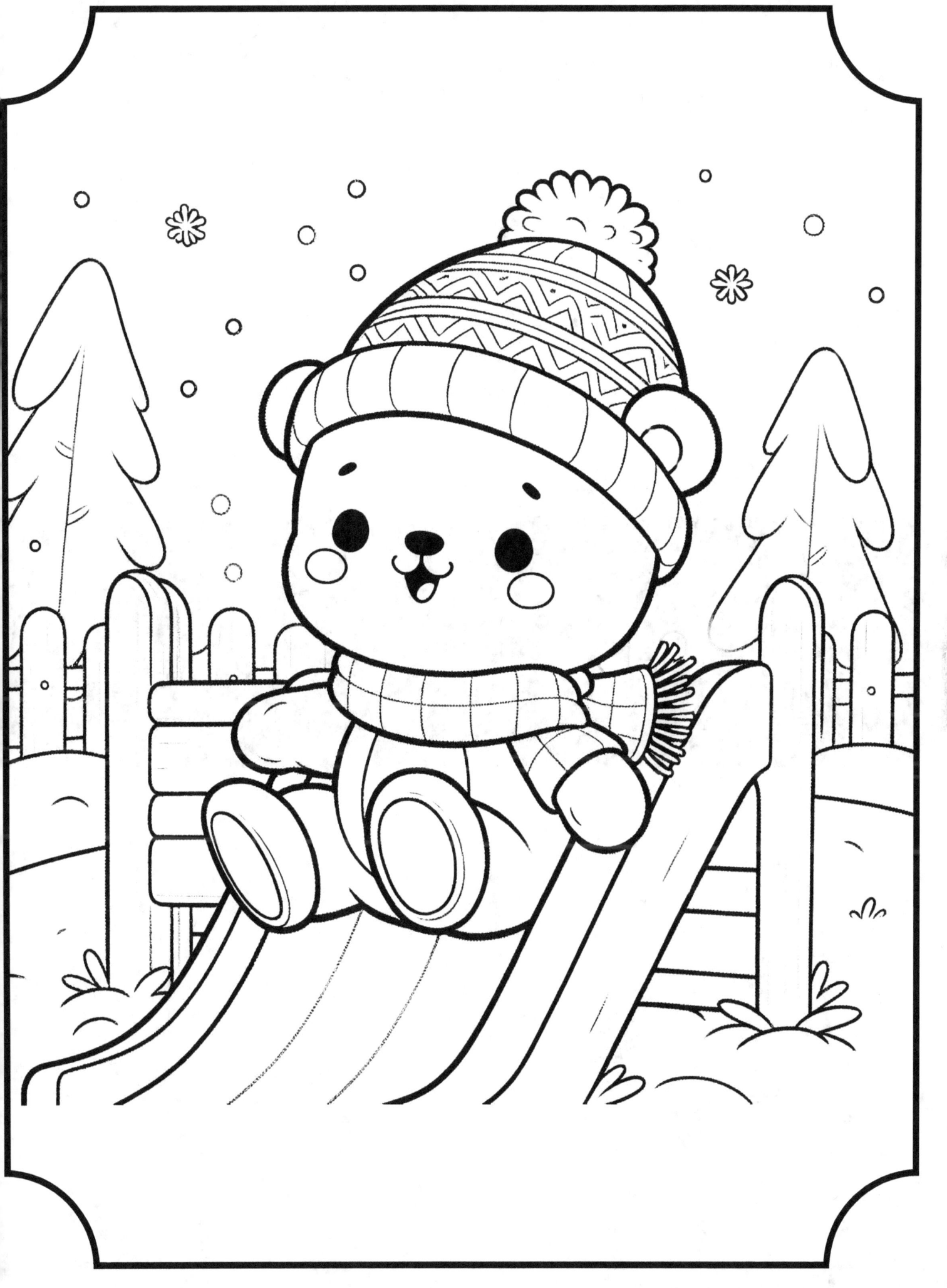

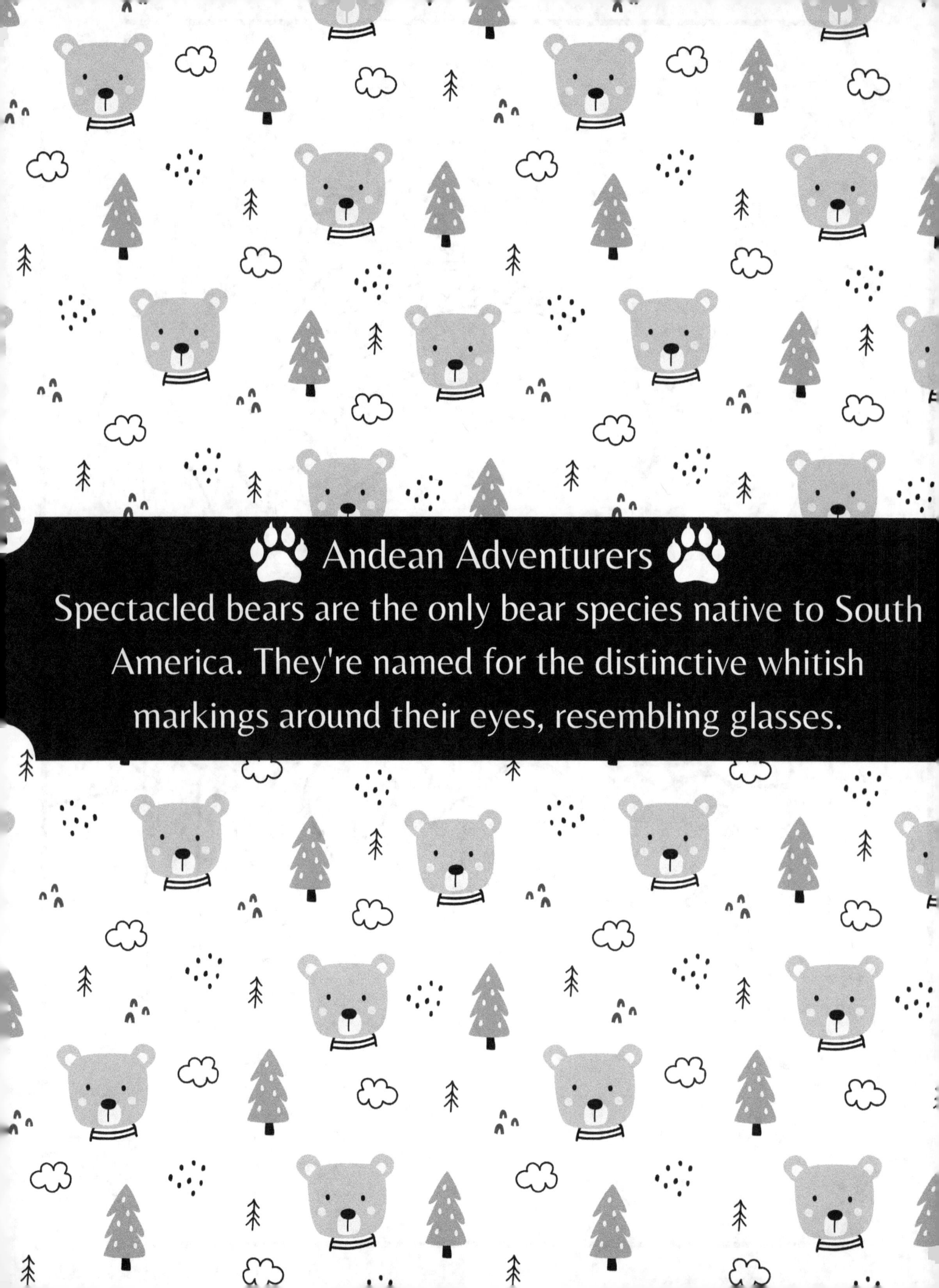

🐾 Andean Adventurers 🐾
Spectacled bears are the only bear species native to South America. They're named for the distinctive whitish markings around their eyes, resembling glasses.

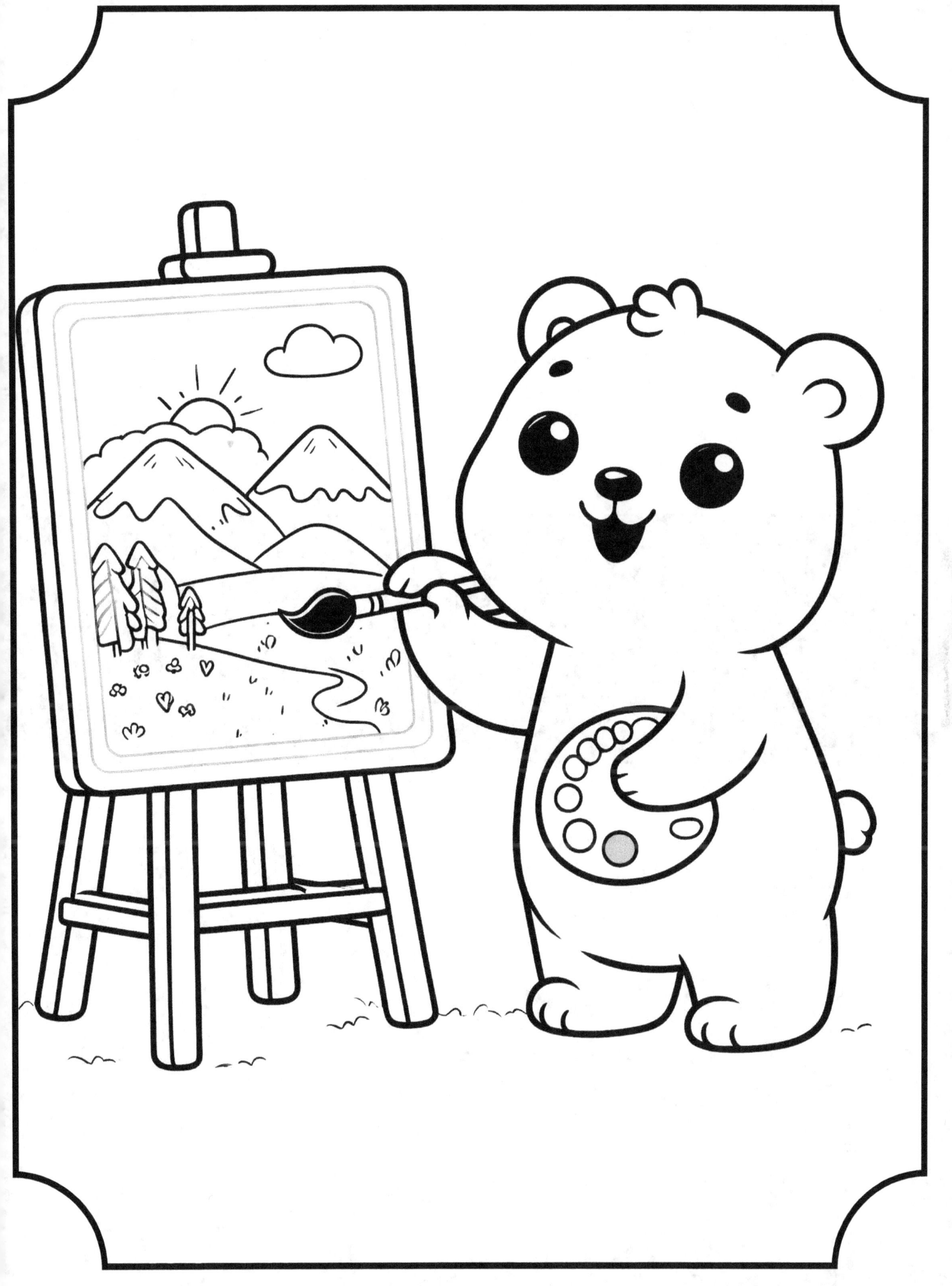

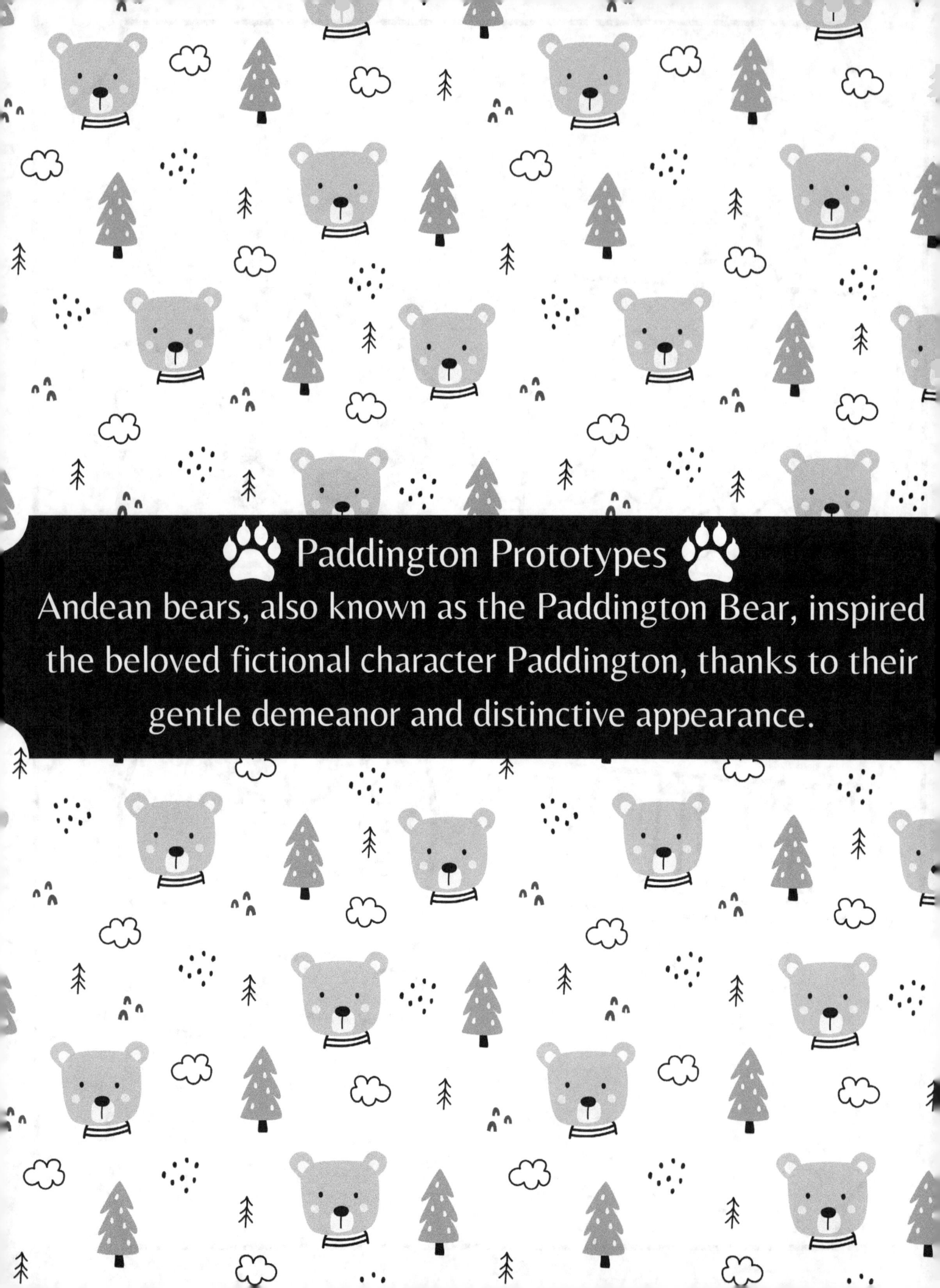

🐾 Paddington Prototypes 🐾
Andean bears, also known as the Paddington Bear, inspired the beloved fictional character Paddington, thanks to their gentle demeanor and distinctive appearance.

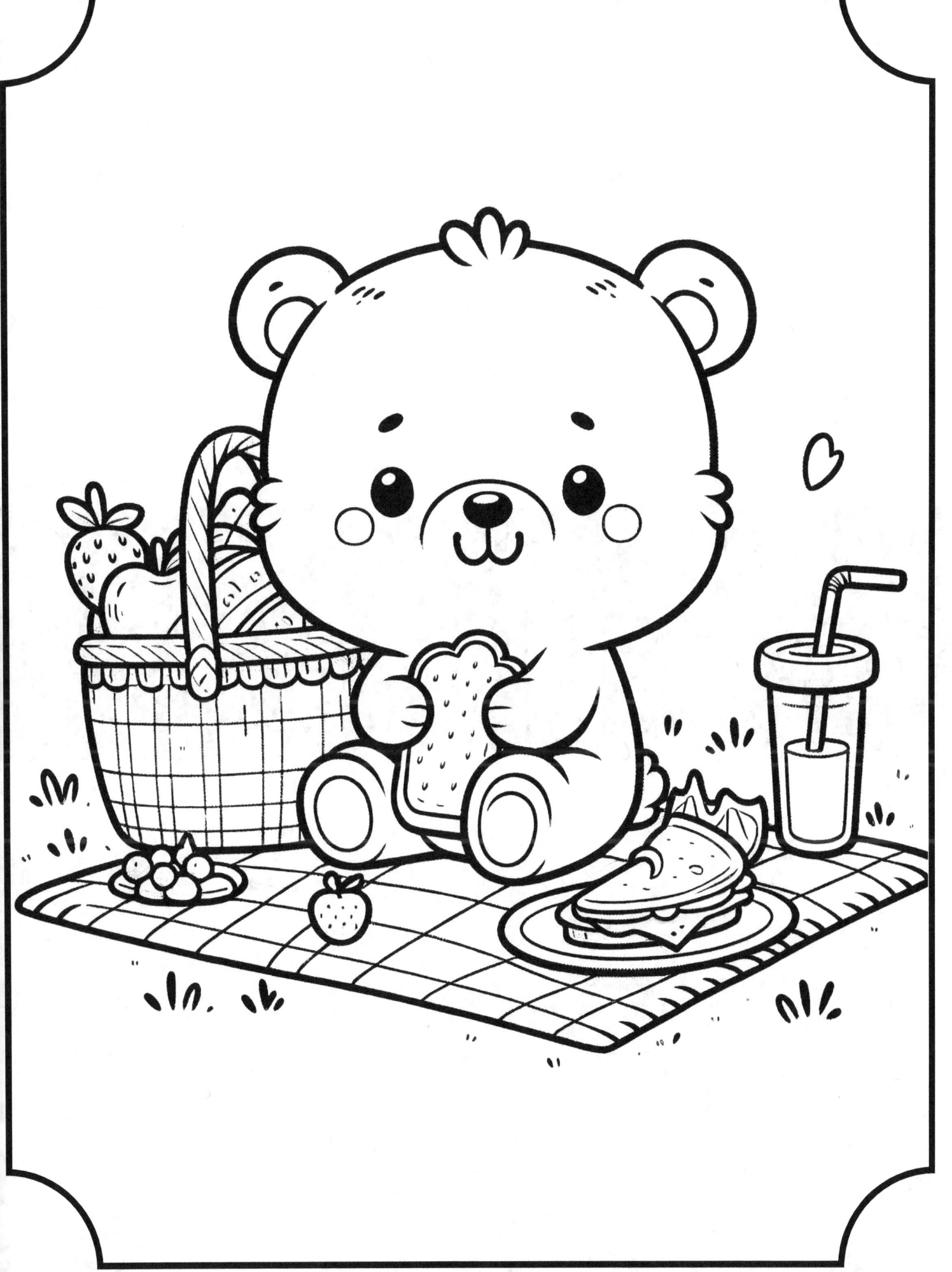

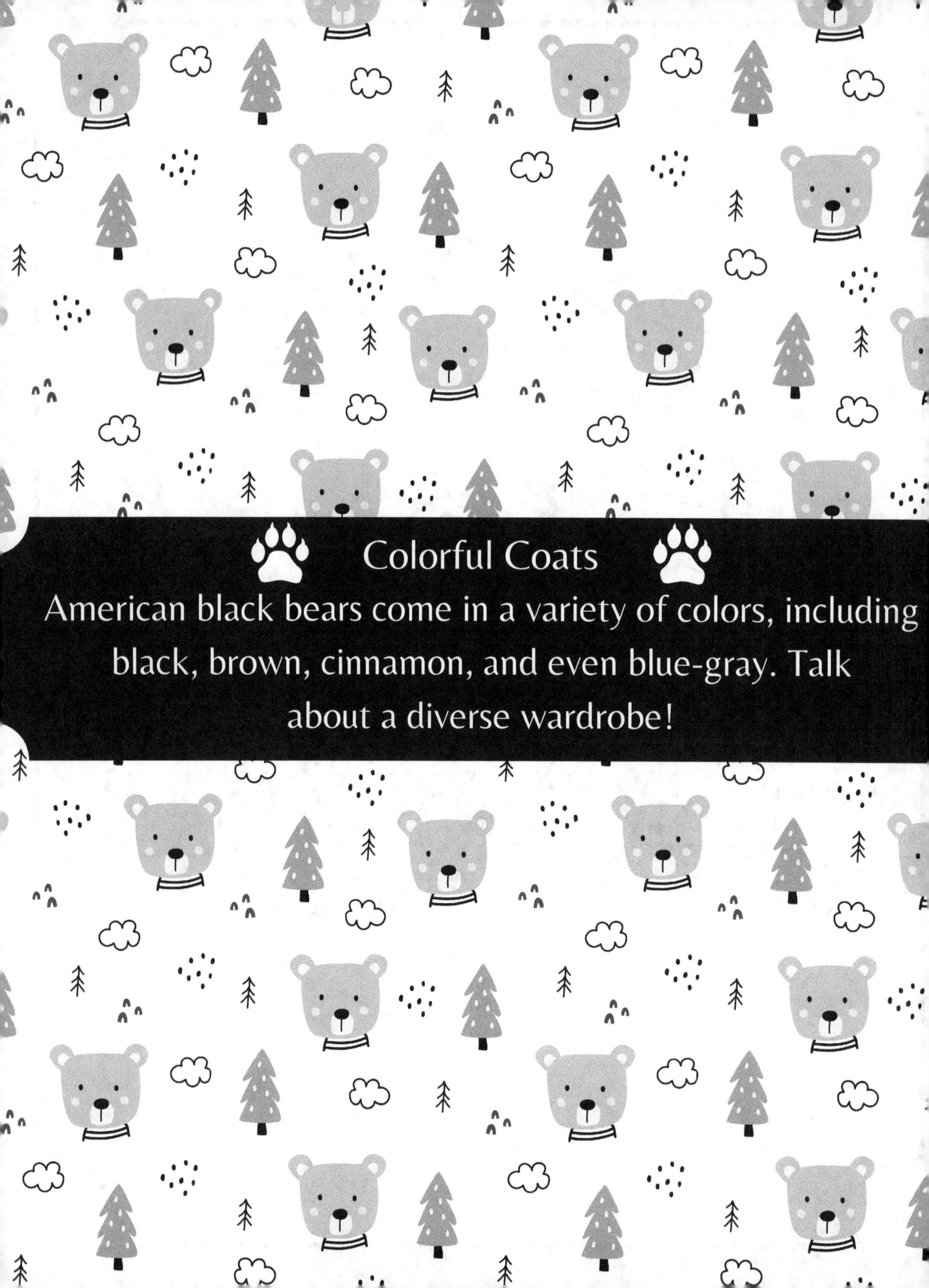

Colorful Coats
American black bears come in a variety of colors, including black, brown, cinnamon, and even blue-gray. Talk about a diverse wardrobe!

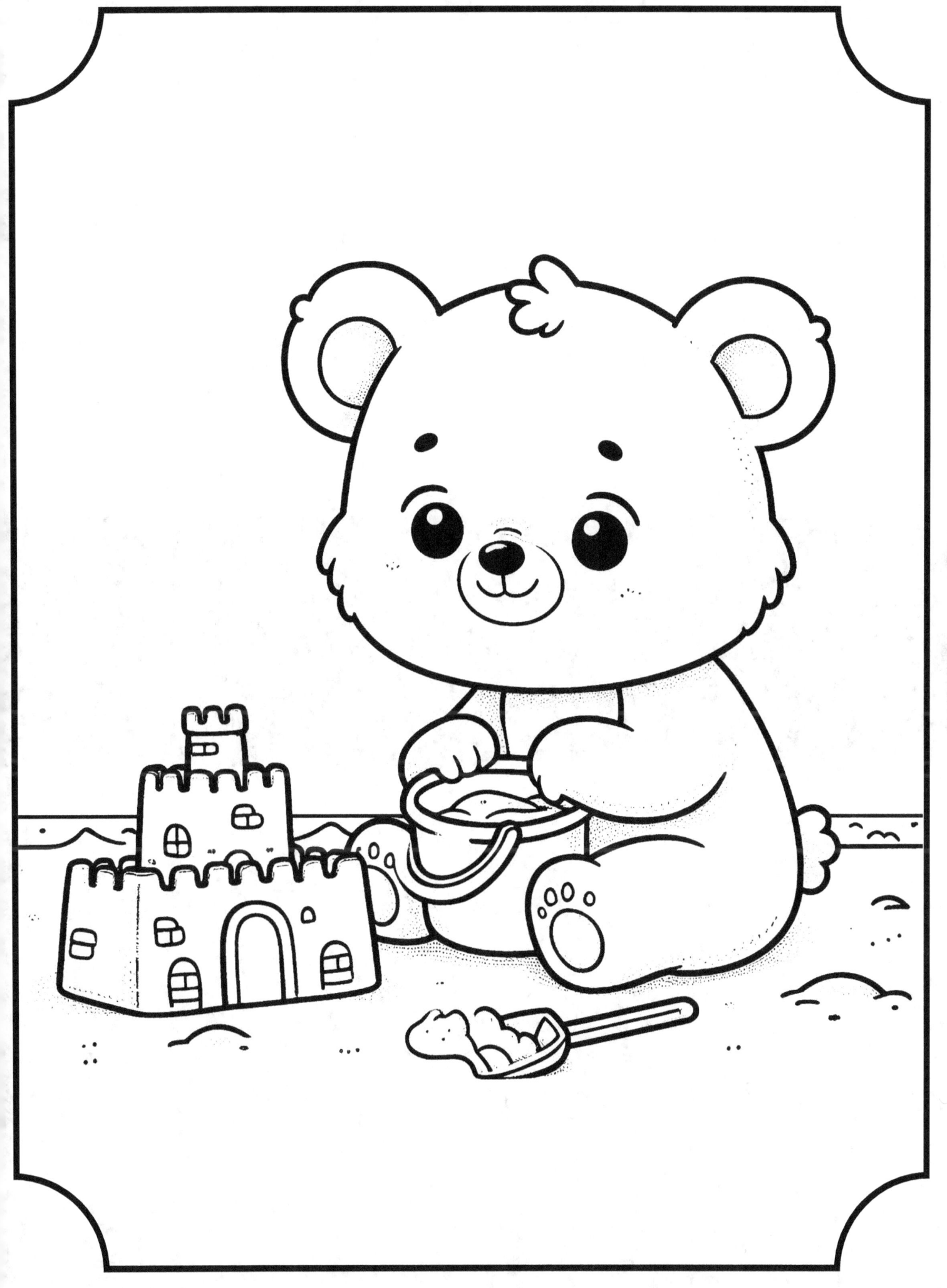

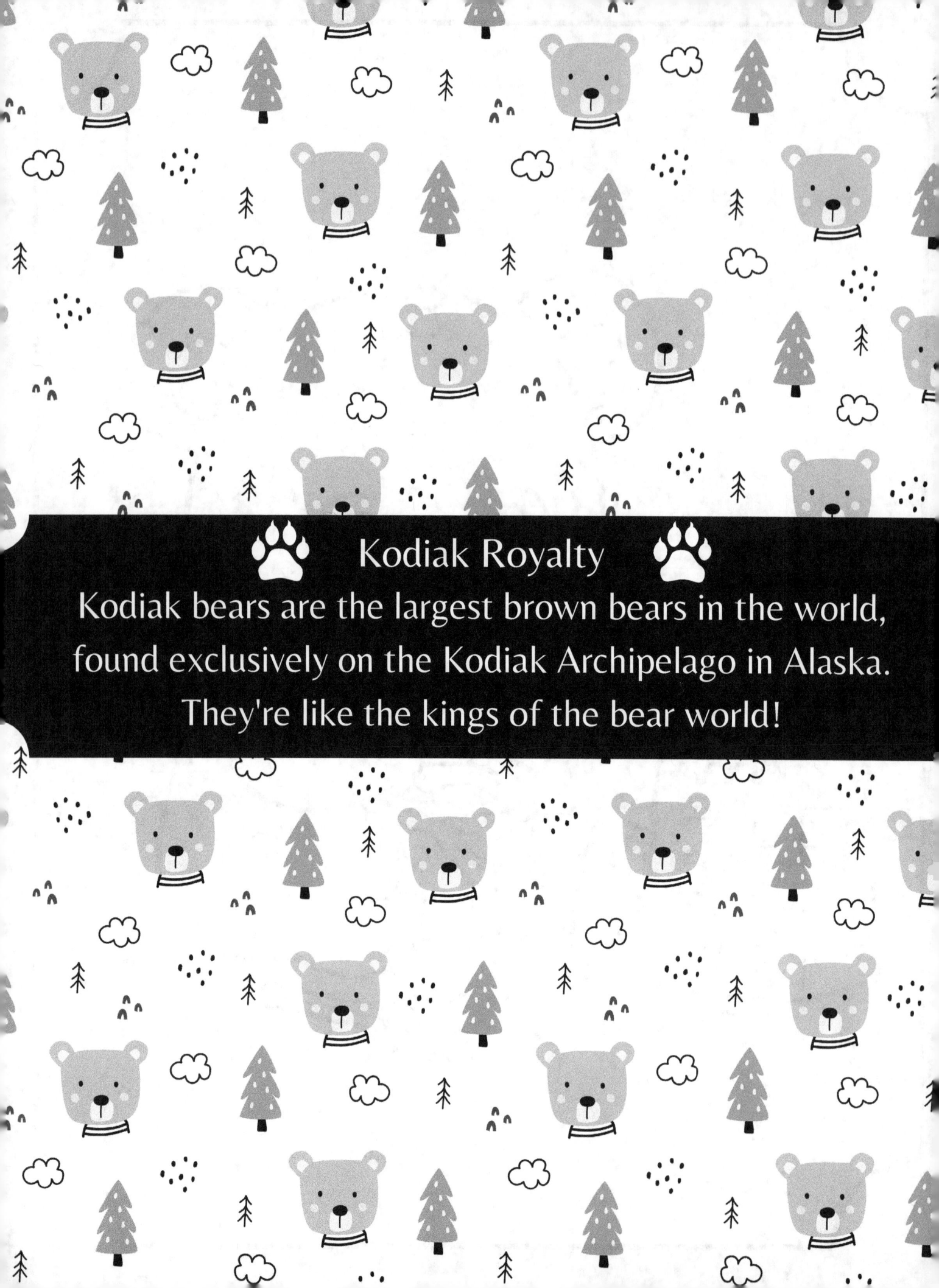

Kodiak Royalty

Kodiak bears are the largest brown bears in the world, found exclusively on the Kodiak Archipelago in Alaska. They're like the kings of the bear world!

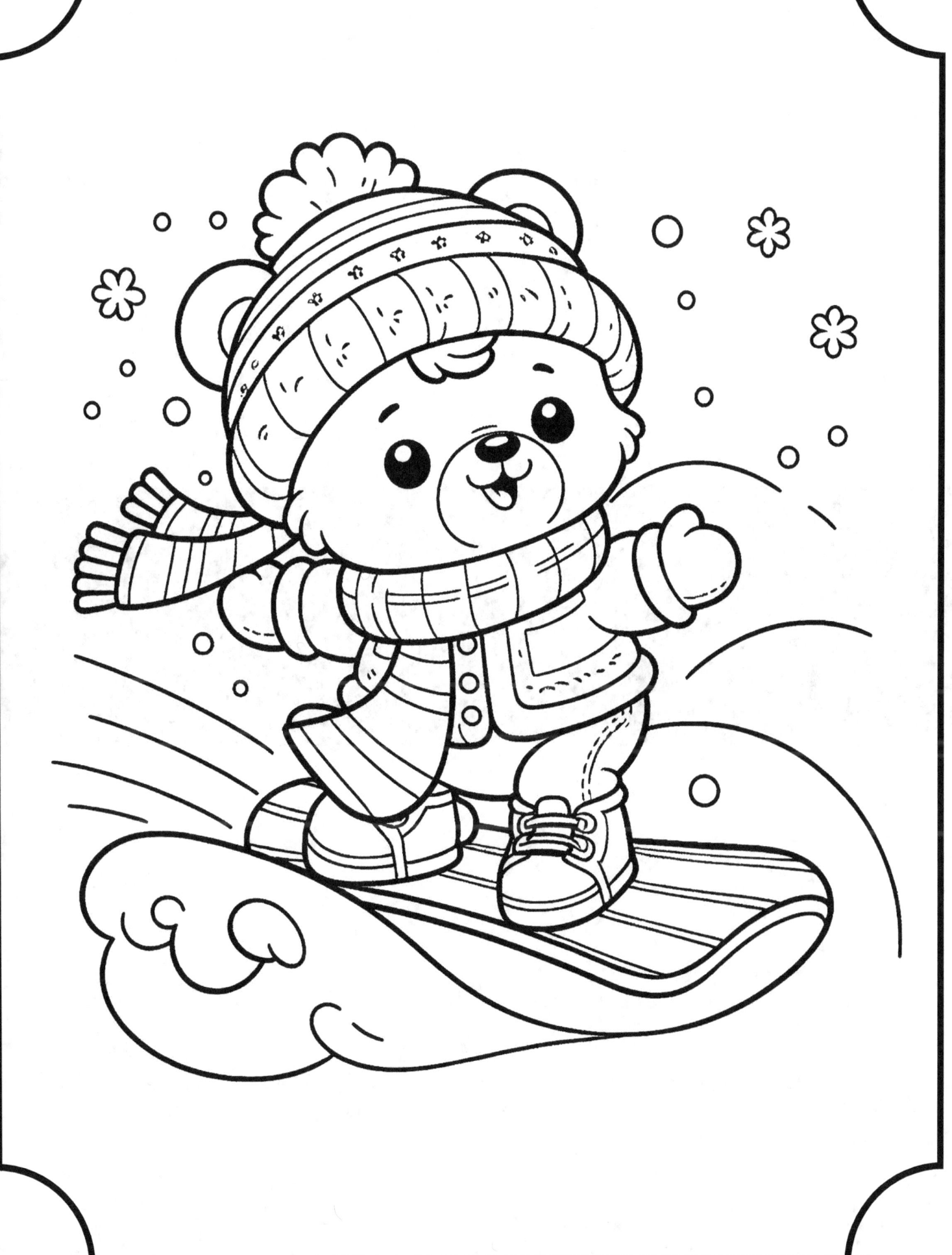

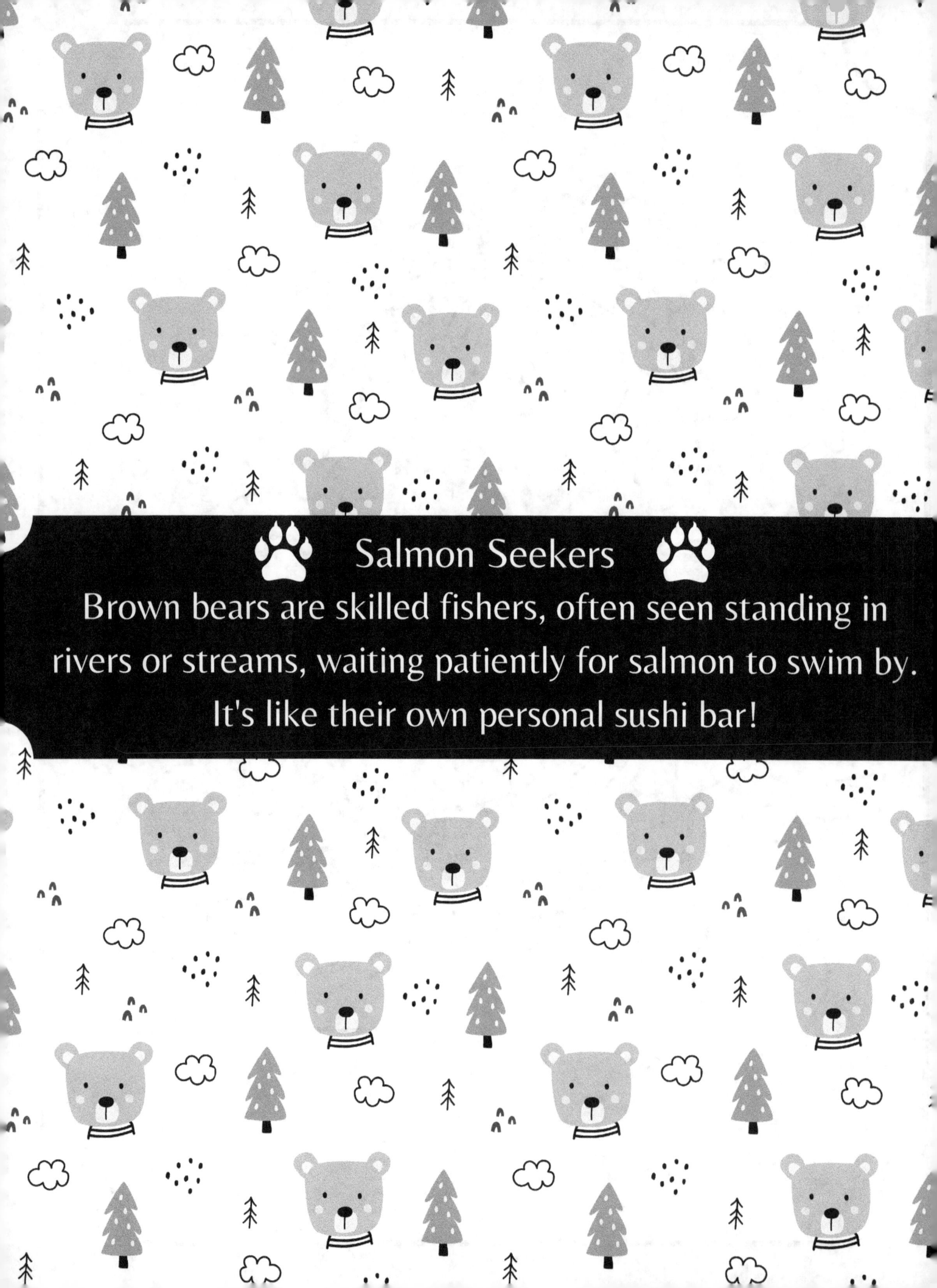

Salmon Seekers

Brown bears are skilled fishers, often seen standing in rivers or streams, waiting patiently for salmon to swim by. It's like their own personal sushi bar!

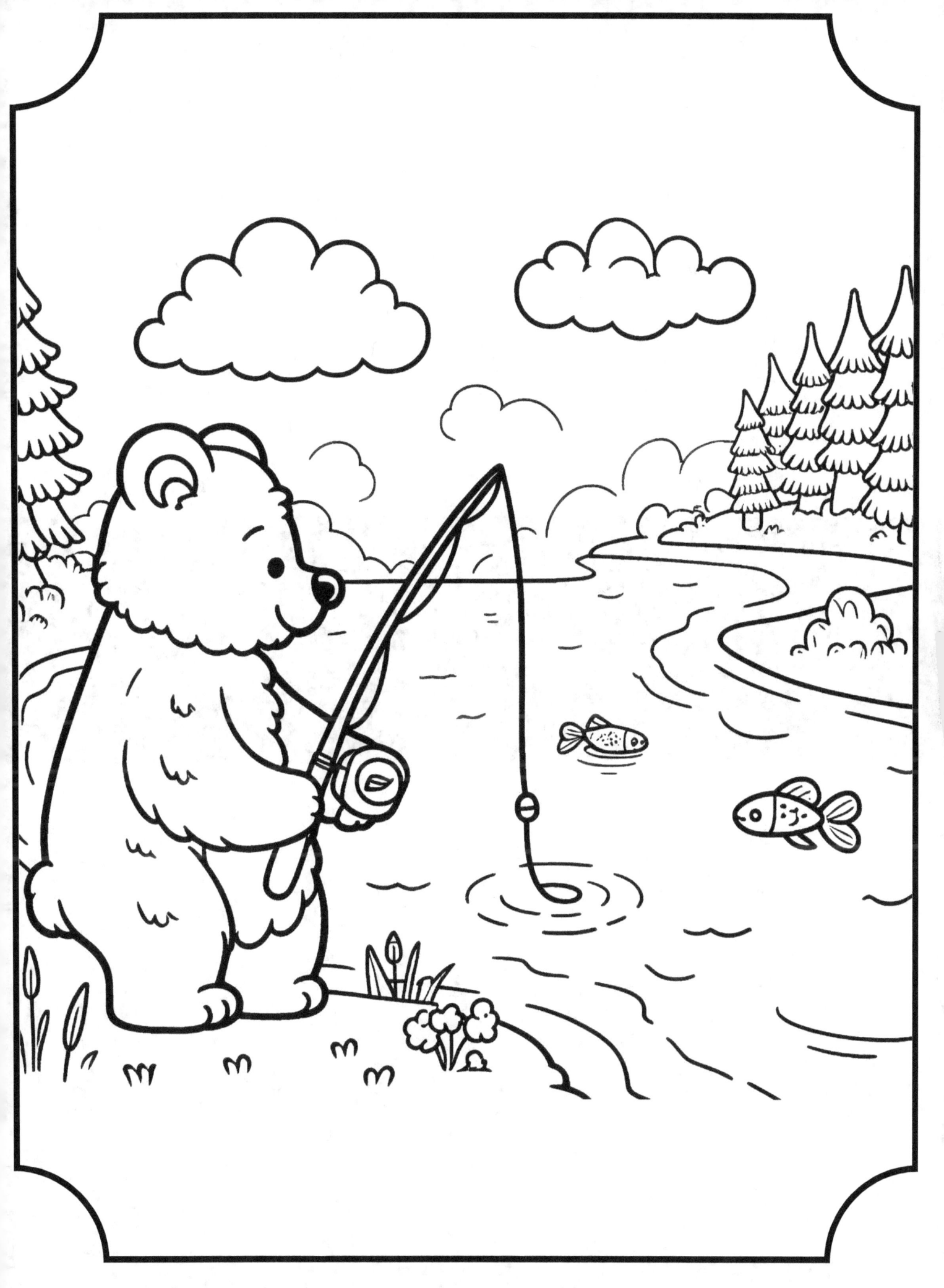

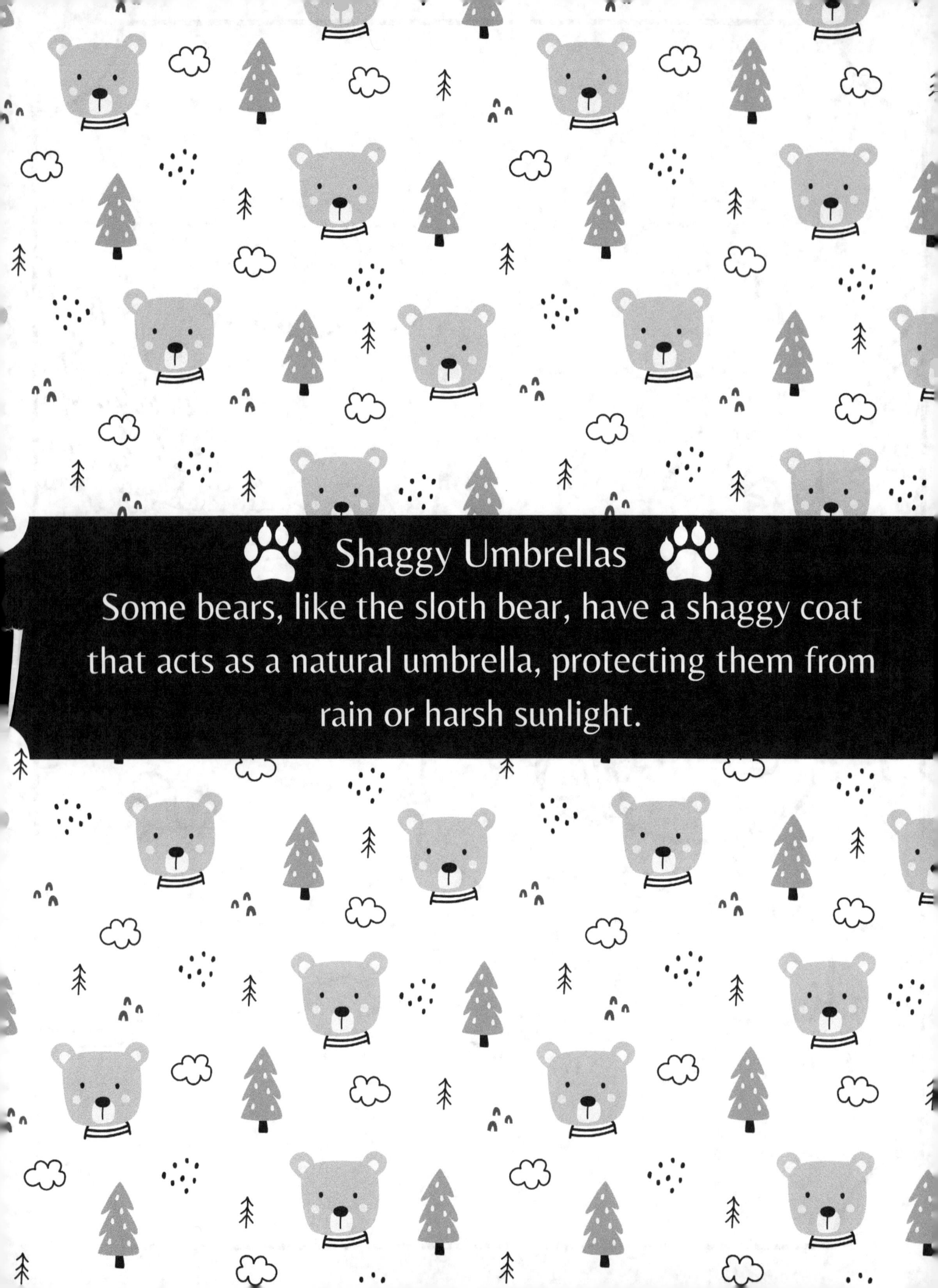

🐾 Shaggy Umbrellas 🐾
Some bears, like the sloth bear, have a shaggy coat that acts as a natural umbrella, protecting them from rain or harsh sunlight.

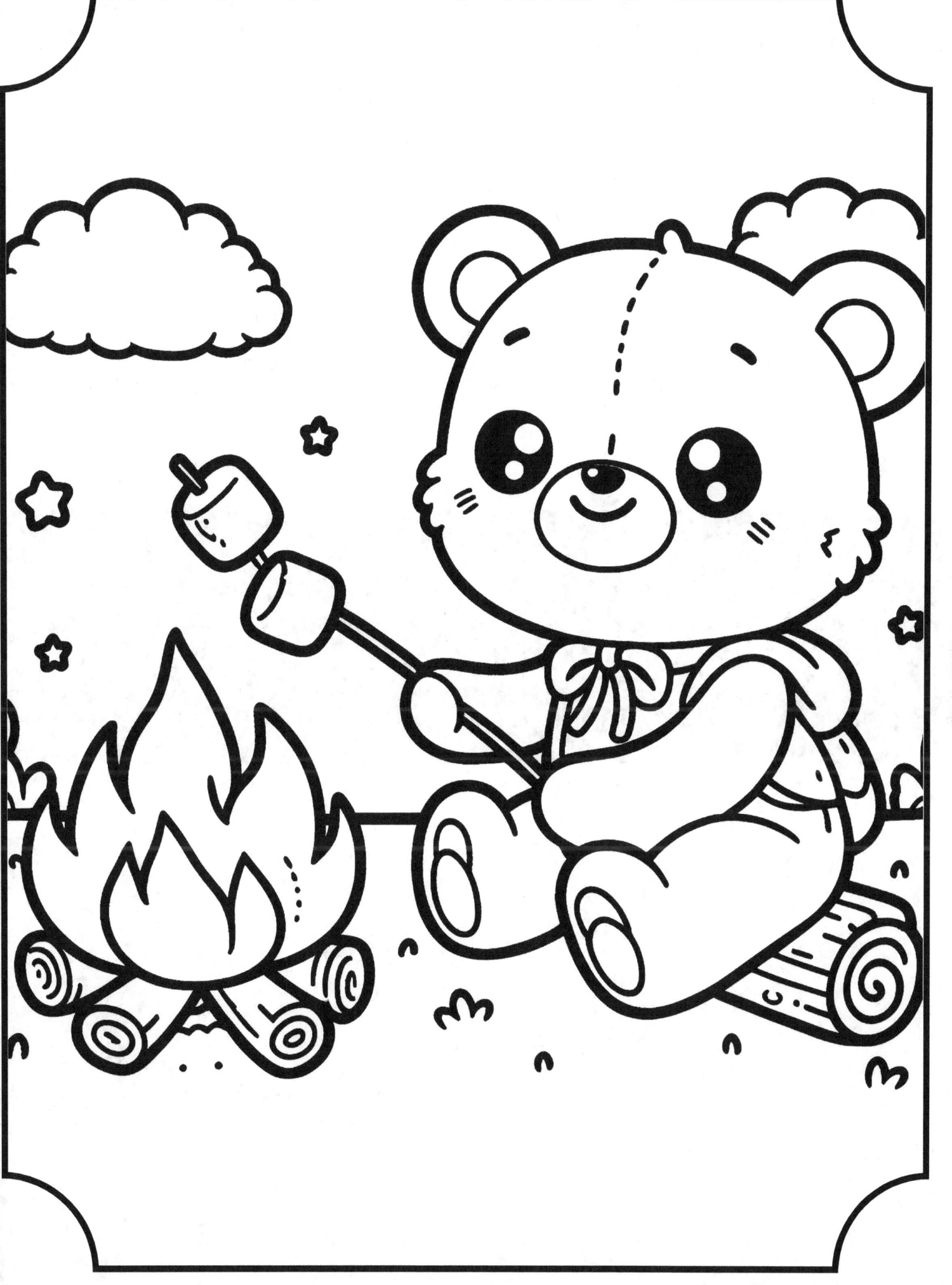

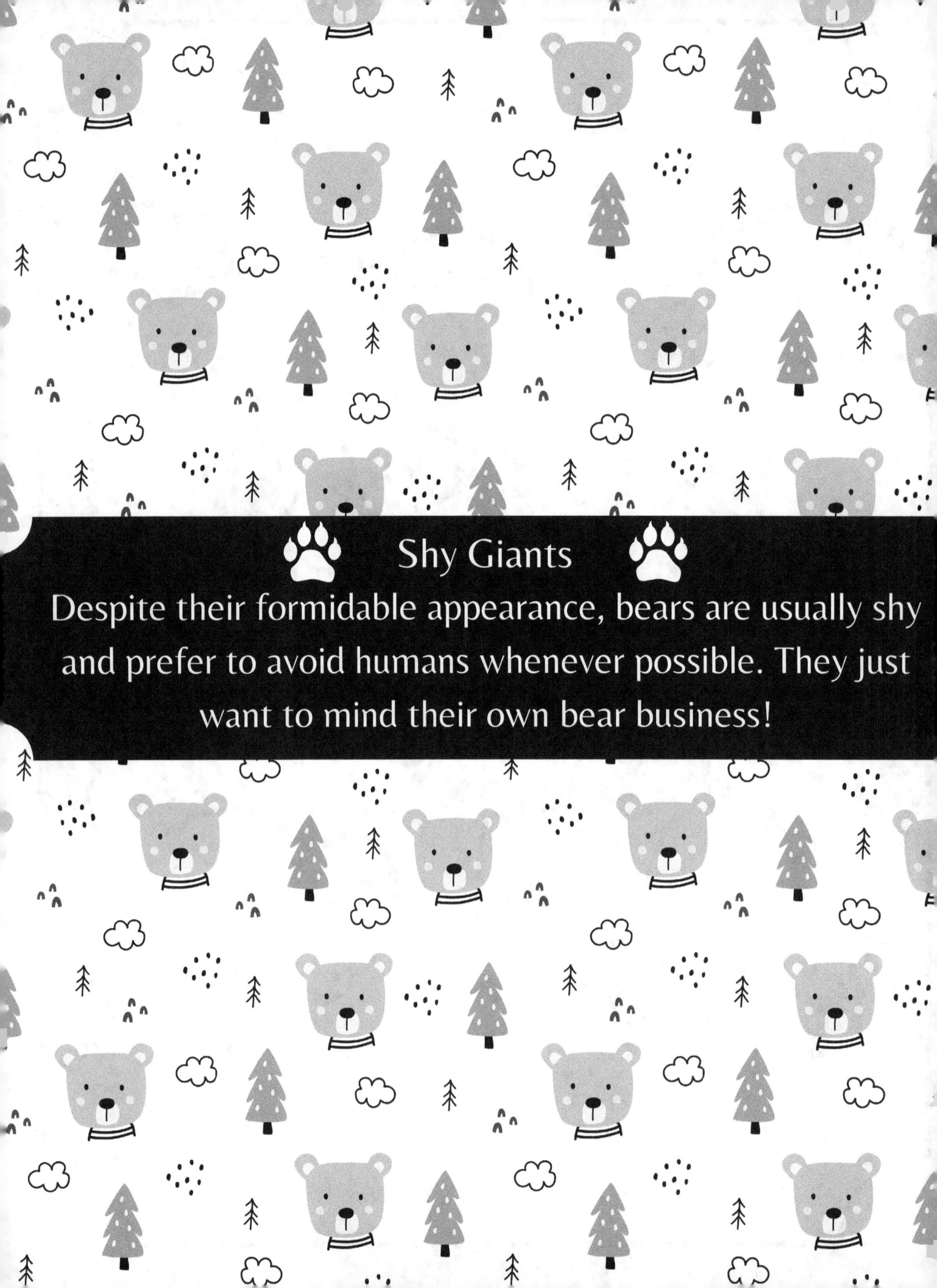

Shy Giants
Despite their formidable appearance, bears are usually shy and prefer to avoid humans whenever possible. They just want to mind their own bear business!

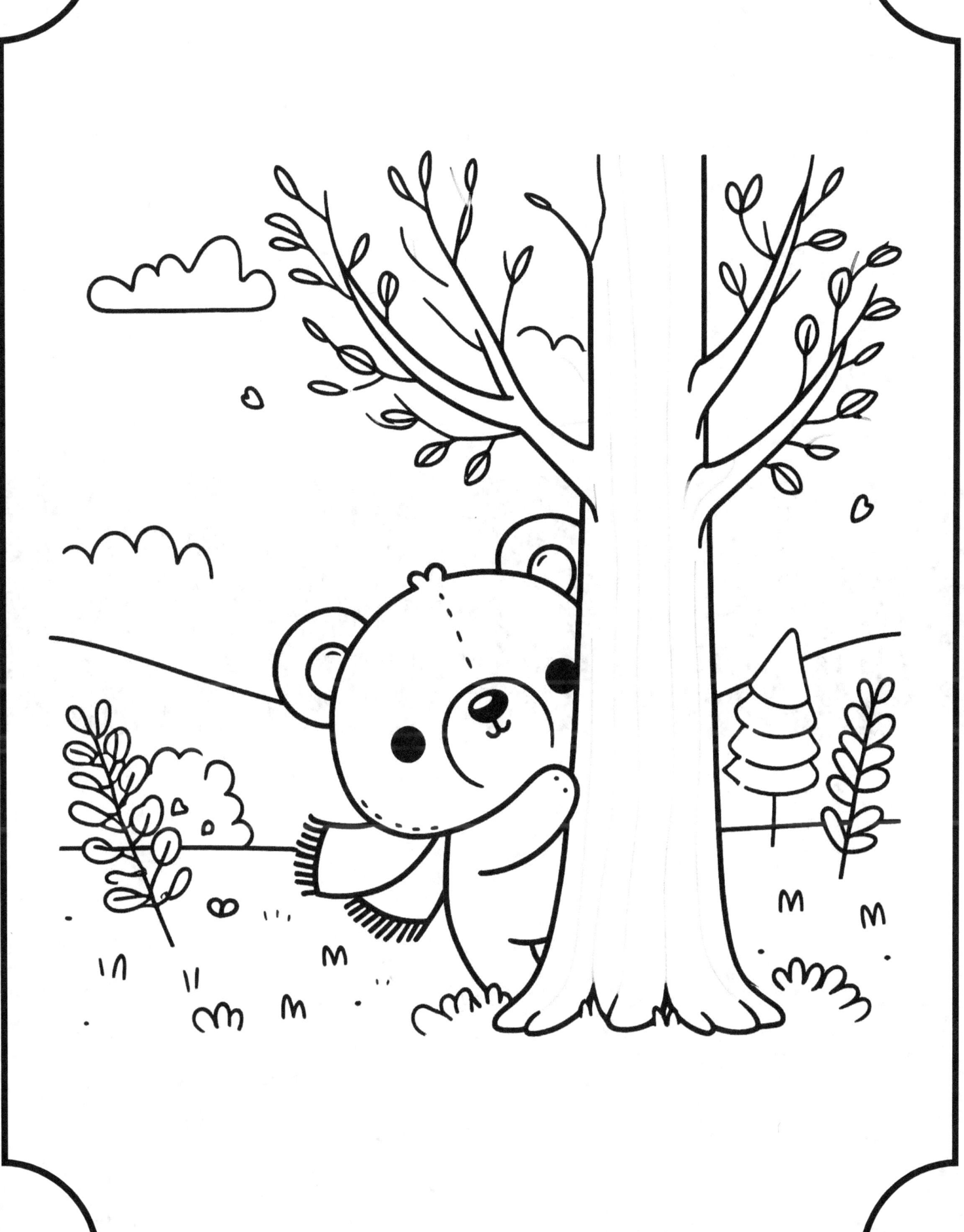

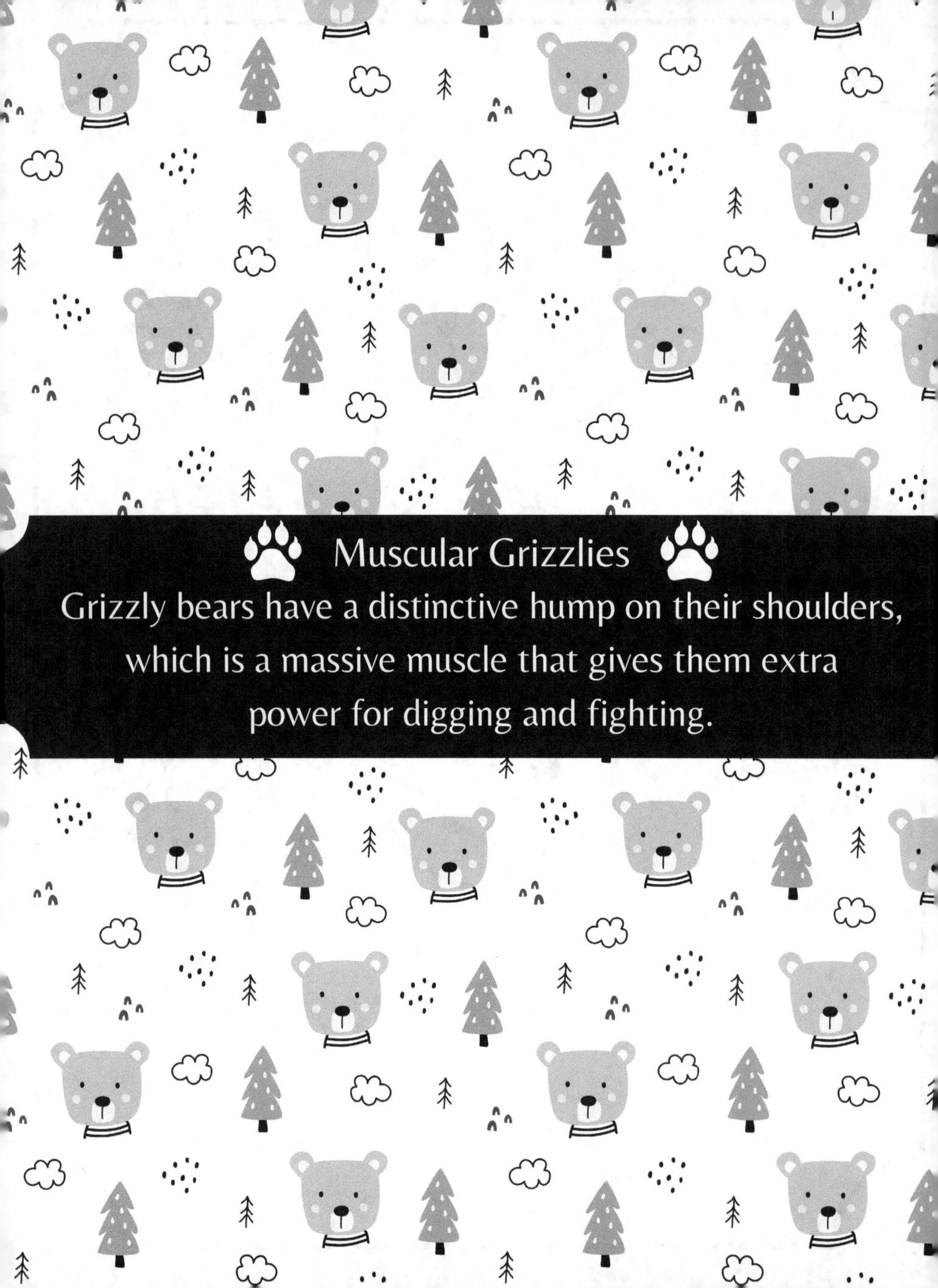

🐾 Muscular Grizzlies 🐾
Grizzly bears have a distinctive hump on their shoulders, which is a massive muscle that gives them extra power for digging and fighting.

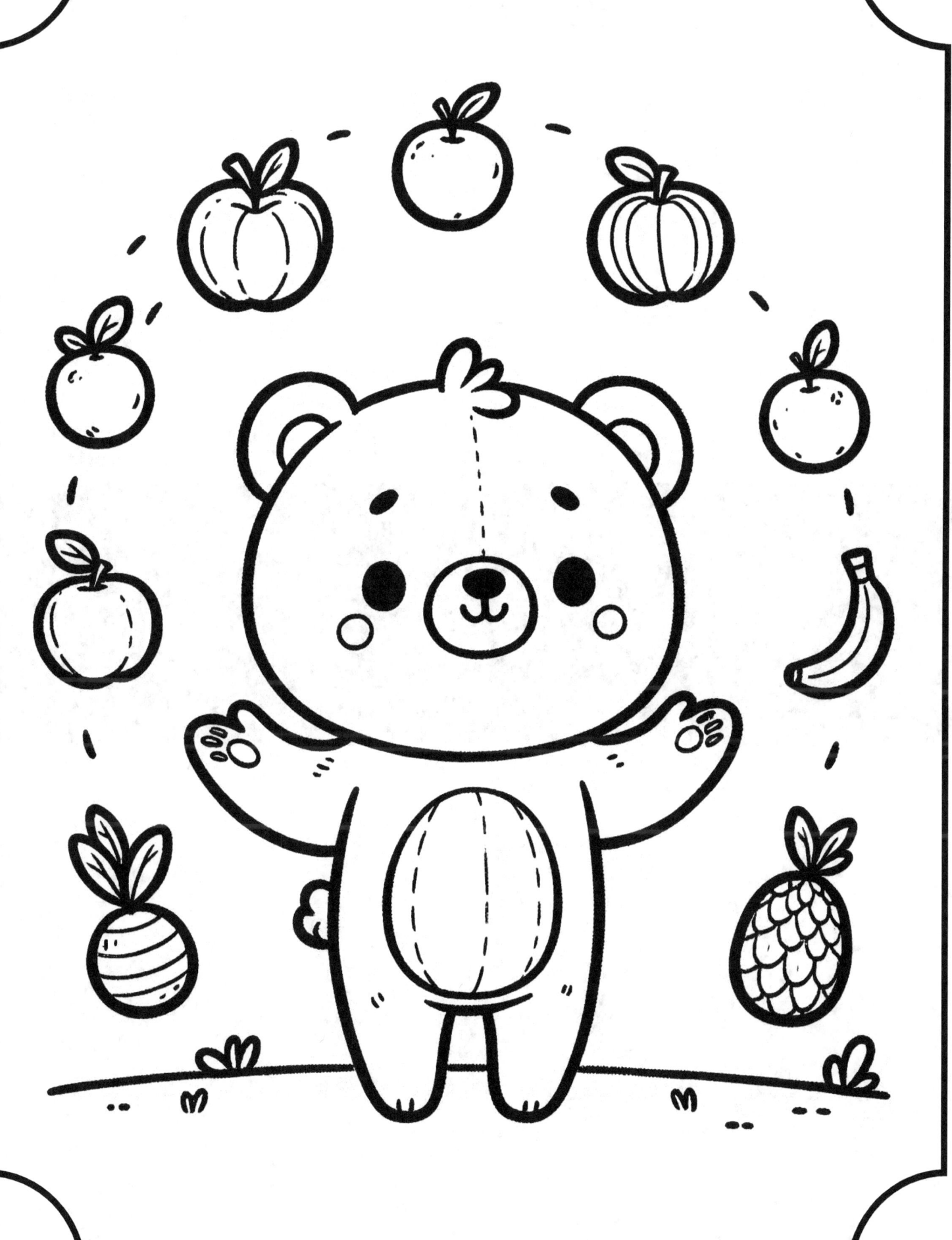

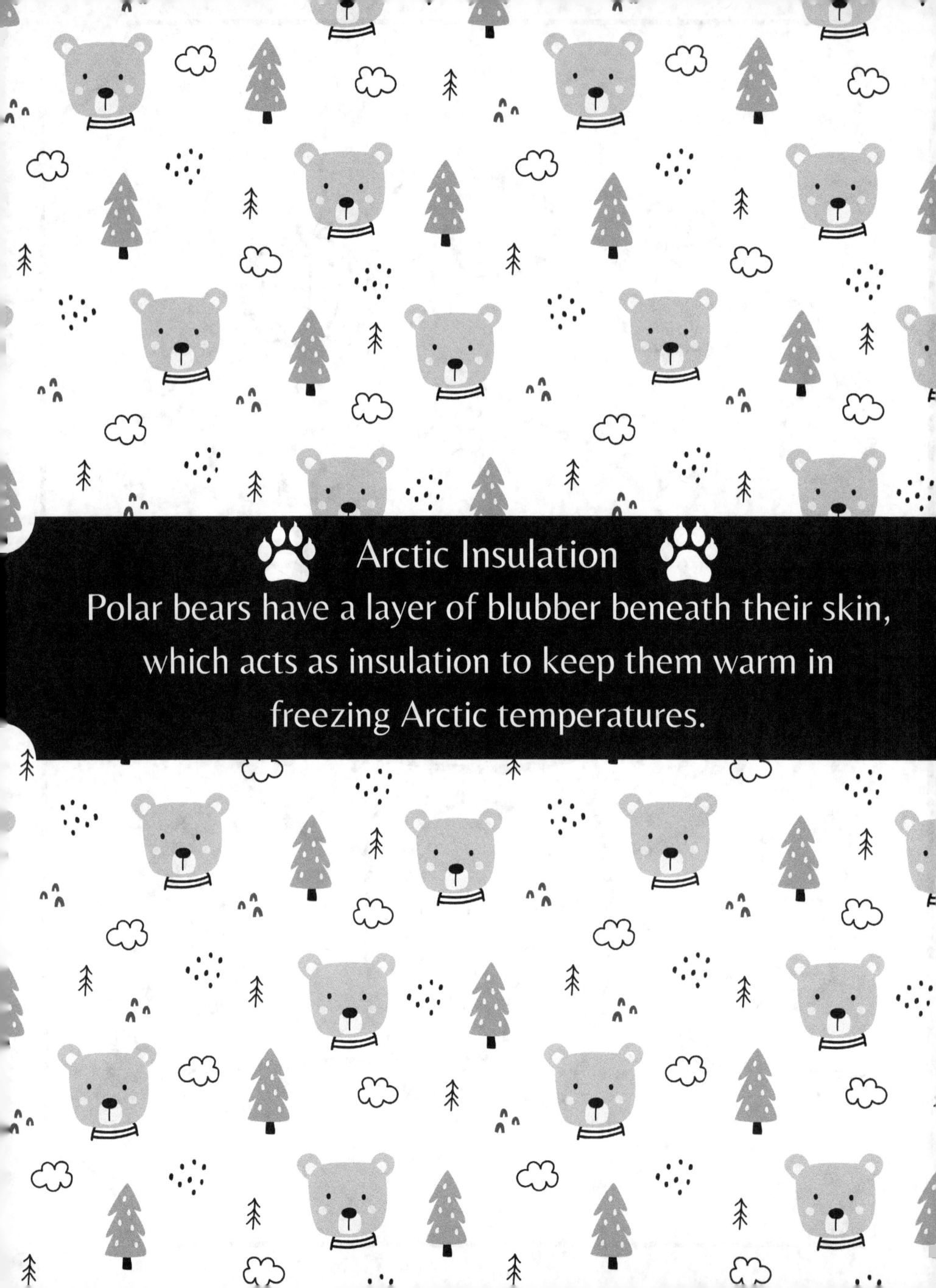

Arctic Insulation
Polar bears have a layer of blubber beneath their skin, which acts as insulation to keep them warm in freezing Arctic temperatures.

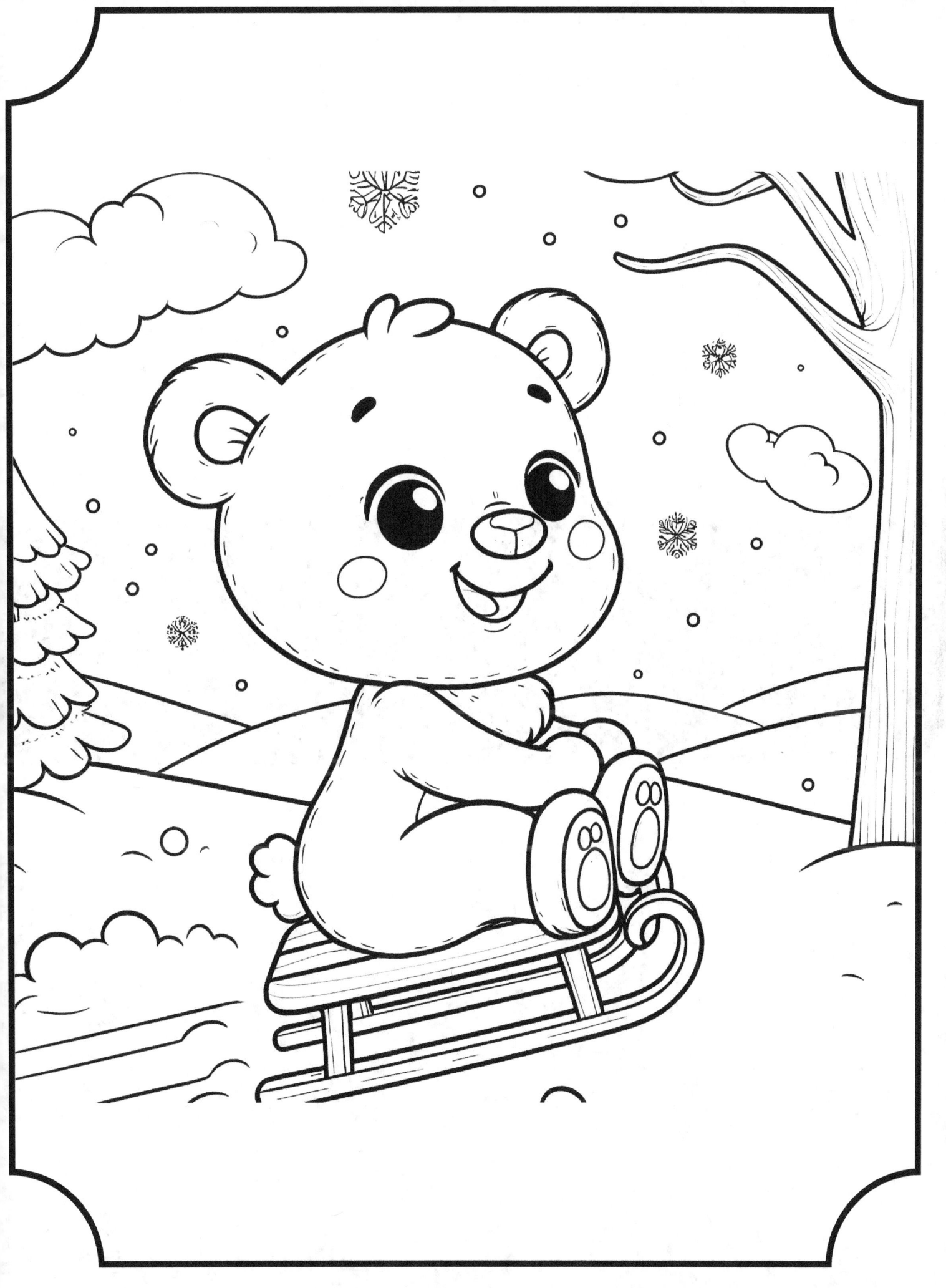

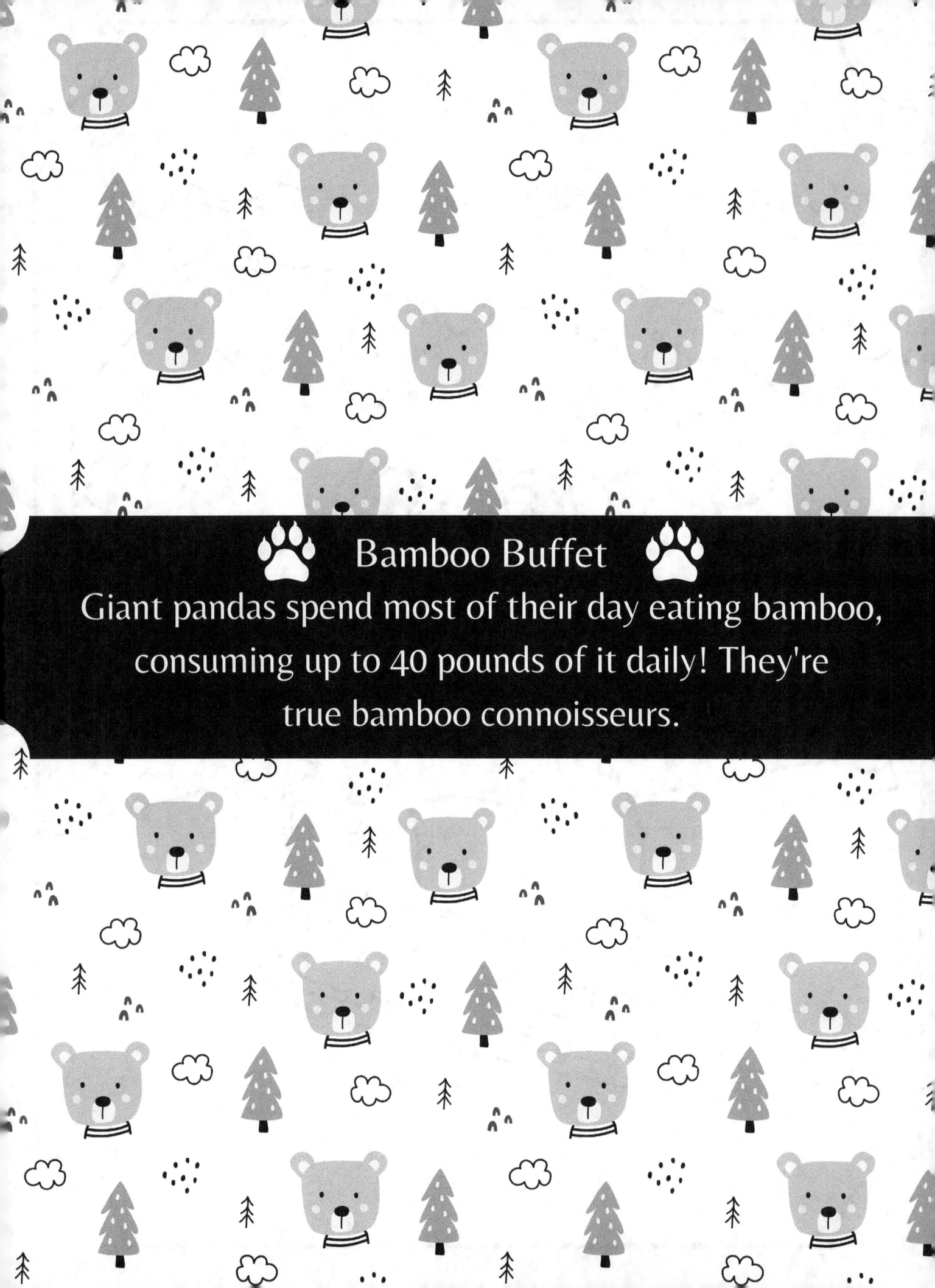

Bamboo Buffet
Giant pandas spend most of their day eating bamboo, consuming up to 40 pounds of it daily! They're true bamboo connoisseurs.

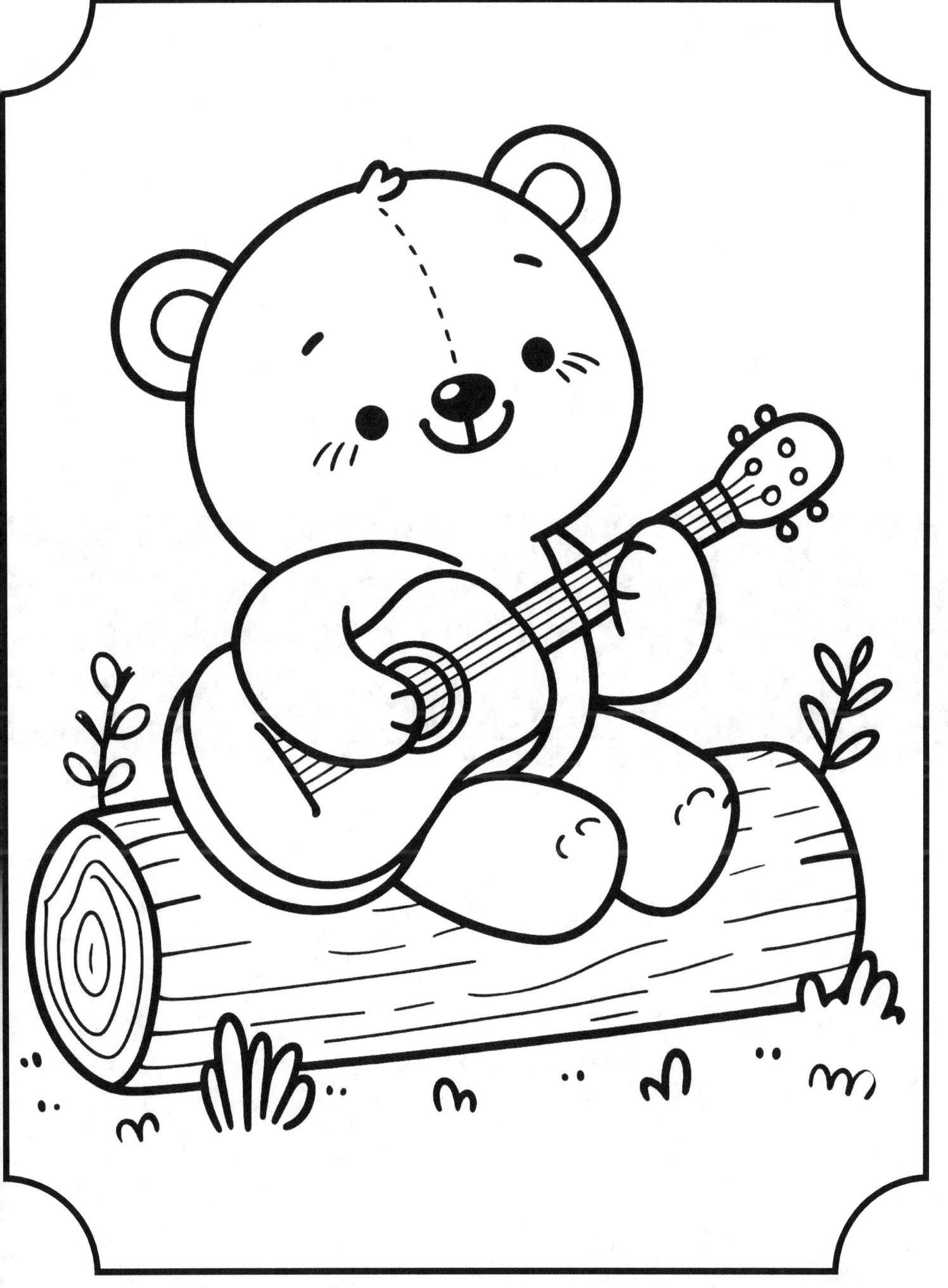

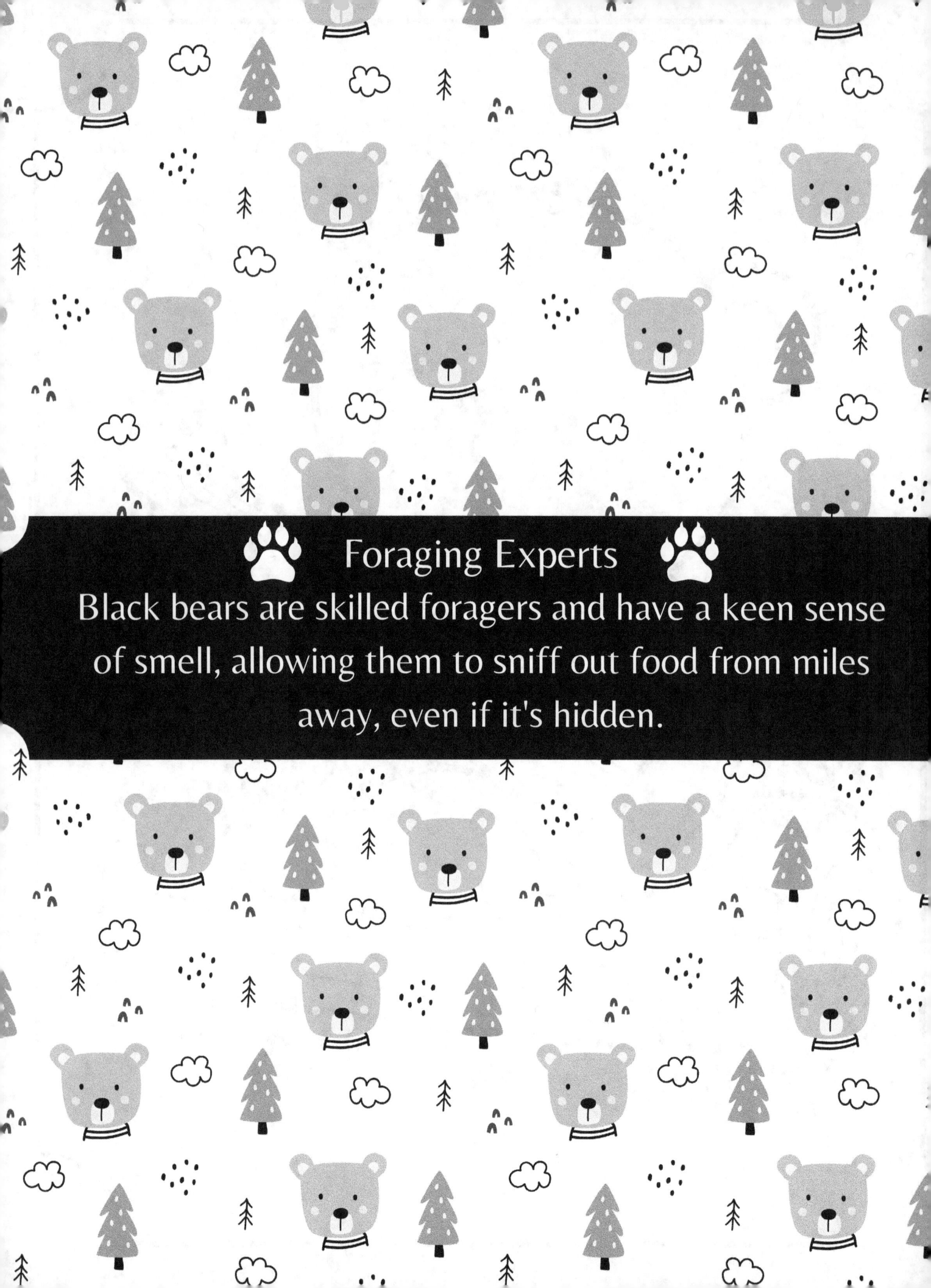

🐾 Foraging Experts 🐾
Black bears are skilled foragers and have a keen sense of smell, allowing them to sniff out food from miles away, even if it's hidden.

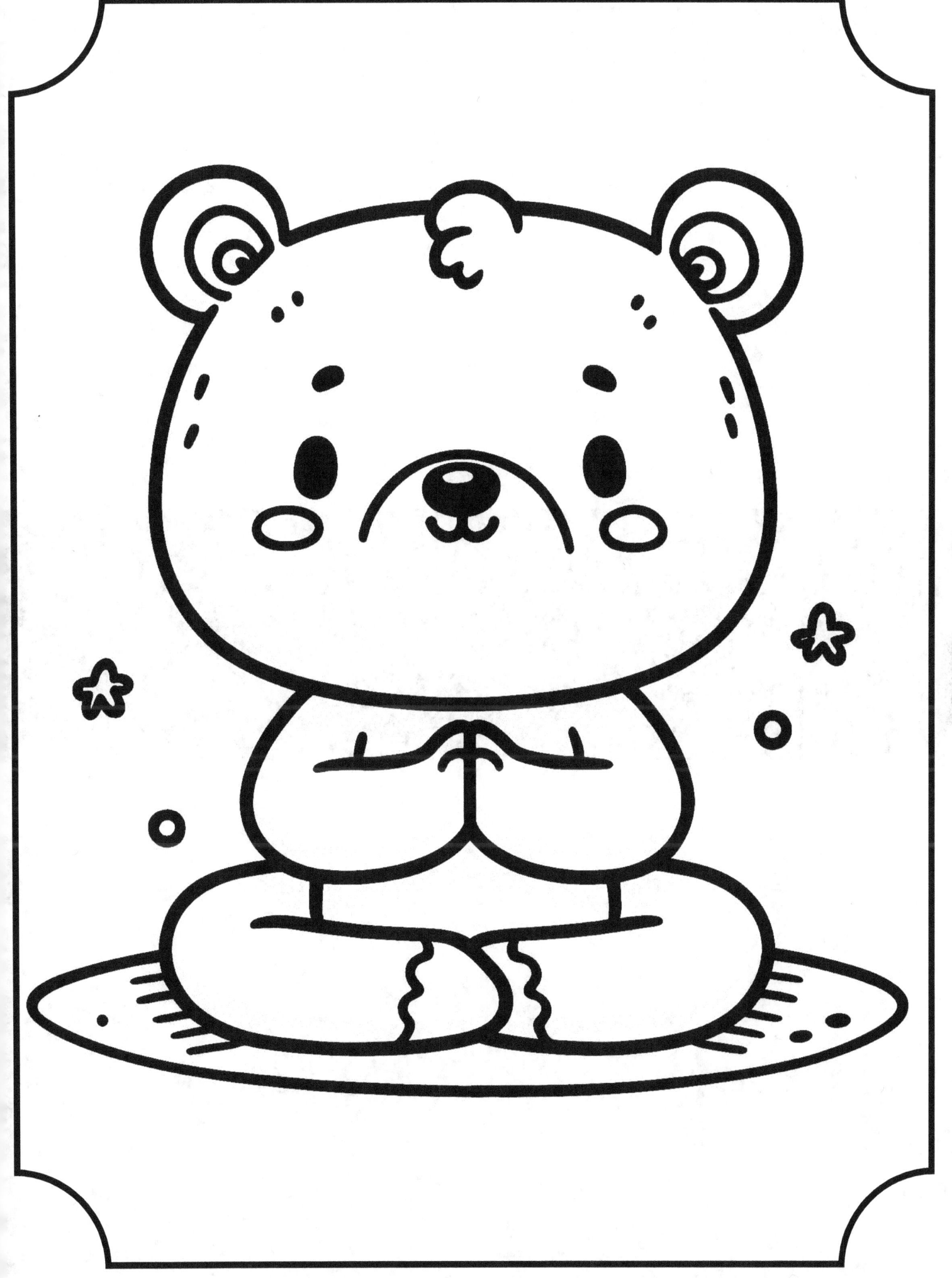

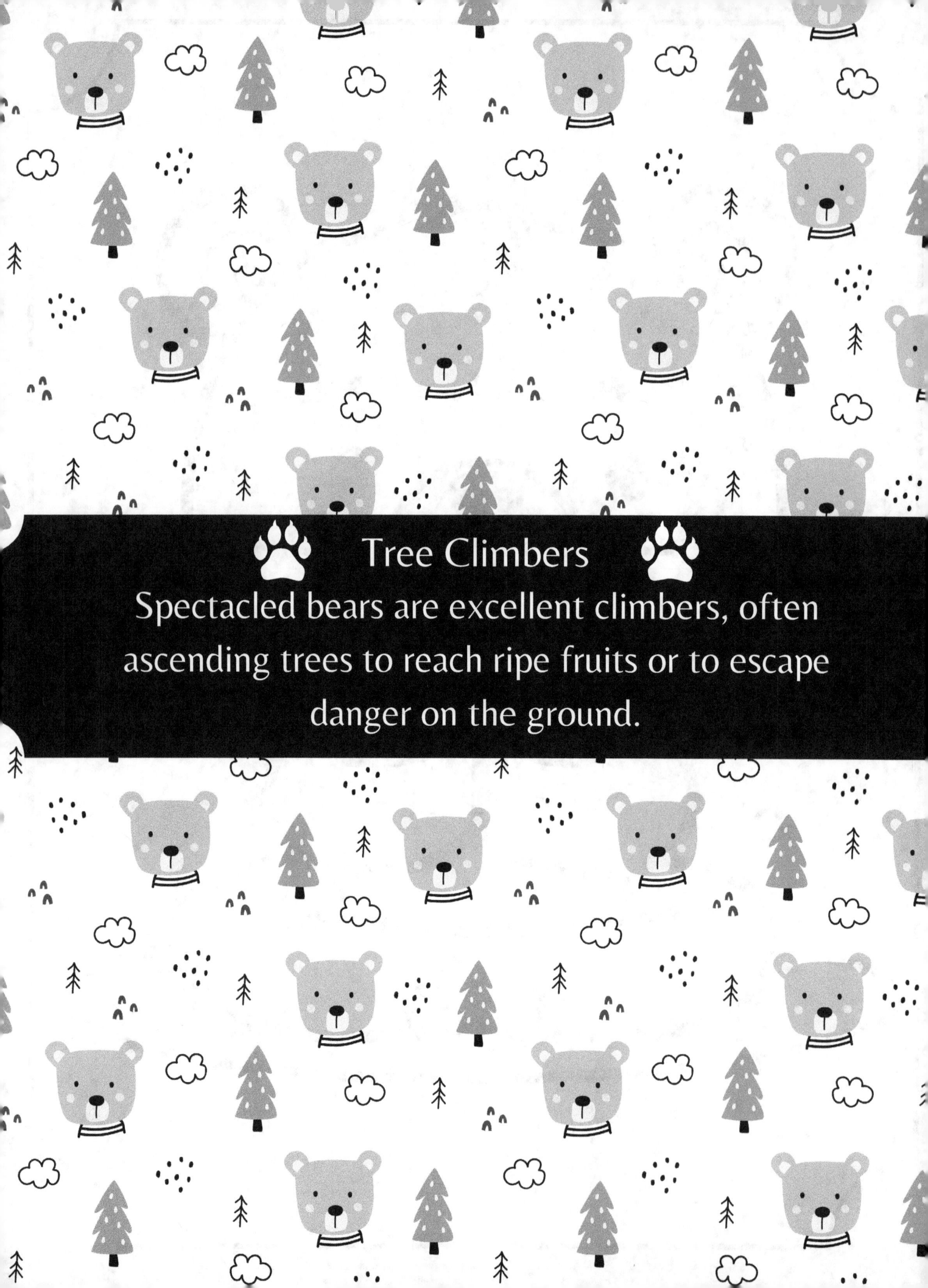

Tree Climbers
Spectacled bears are excellent climbers, often ascending trees to reach ripe fruits or to escape danger on the ground.

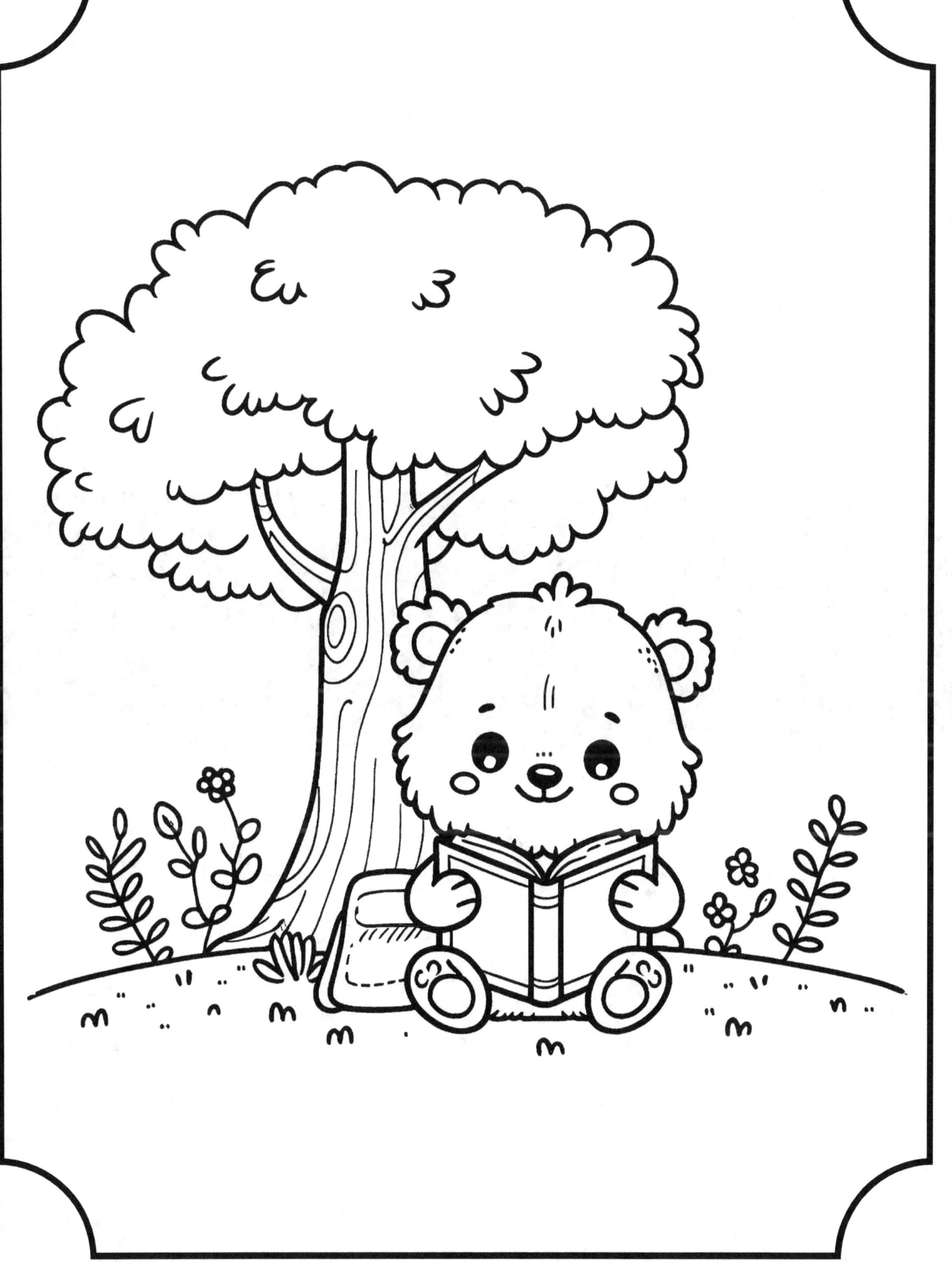

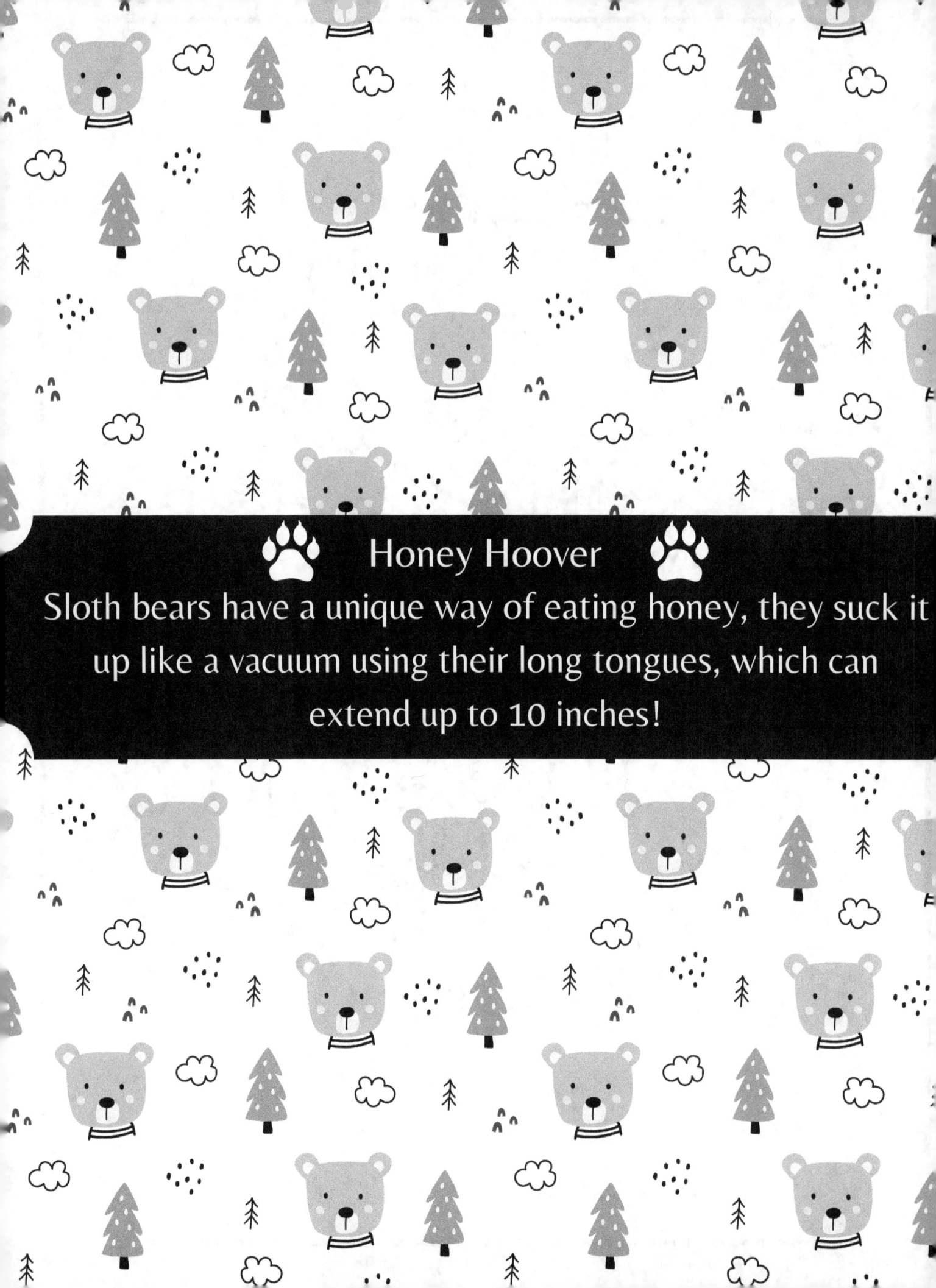

Honey Hoover

Sloth bears have a unique way of eating honey, they suck it up like a vacuum using their long tongues, which can extend up to 10 inches!

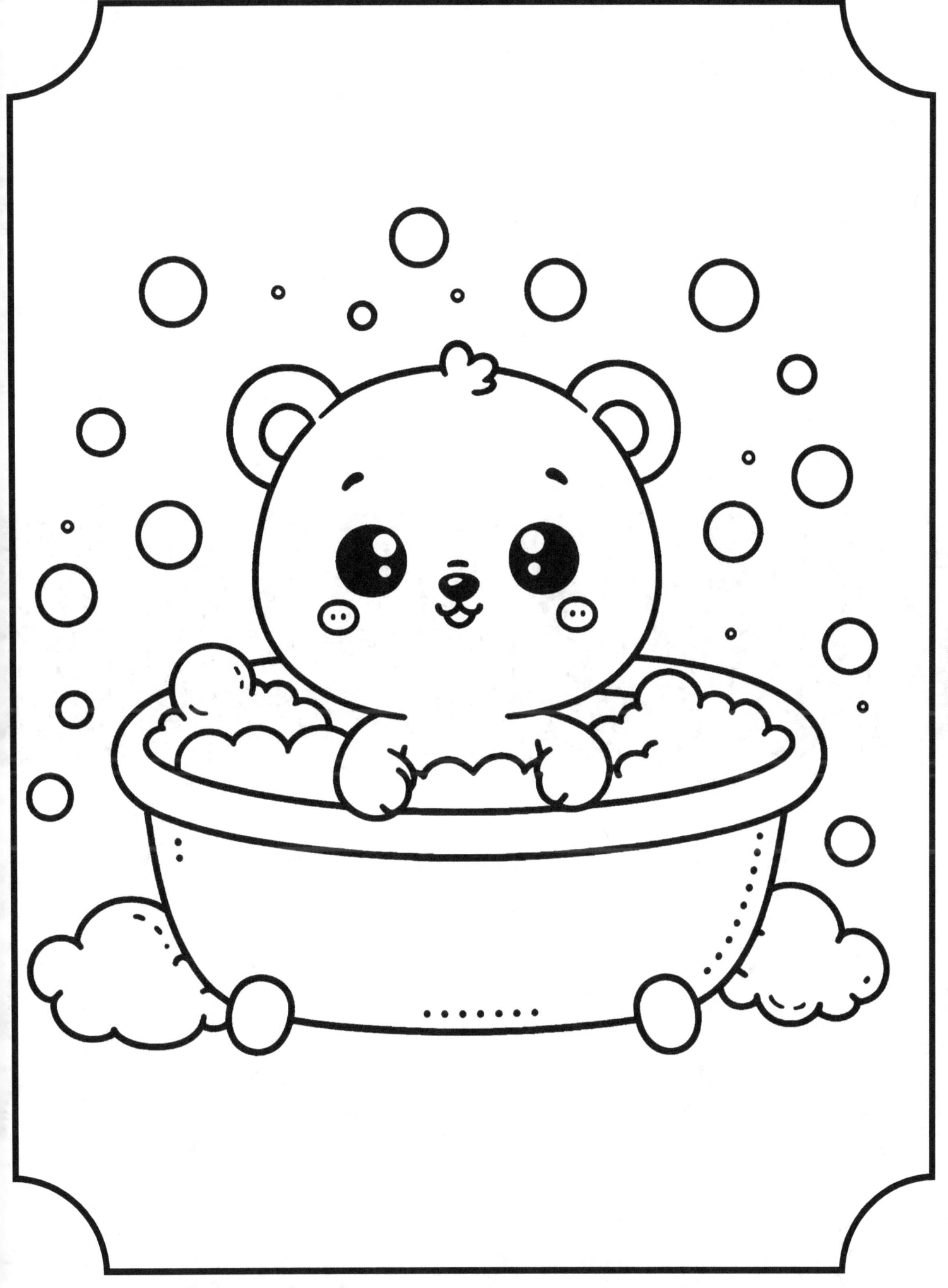

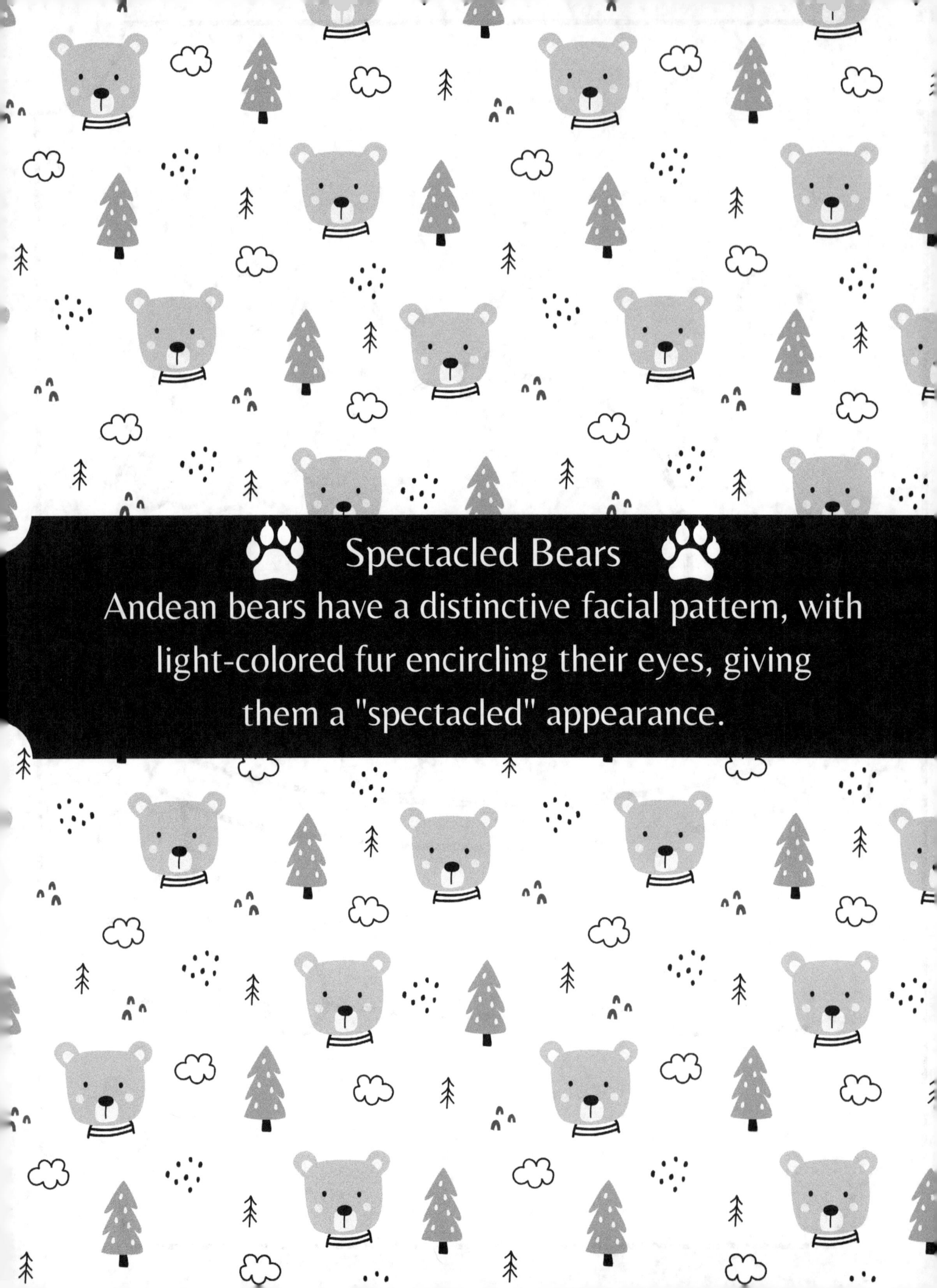

Spectacled Bears

Andean bears have a distinctive facial pattern, with light-colored fur encircling their eyes, giving them a "spectacled" appearance.

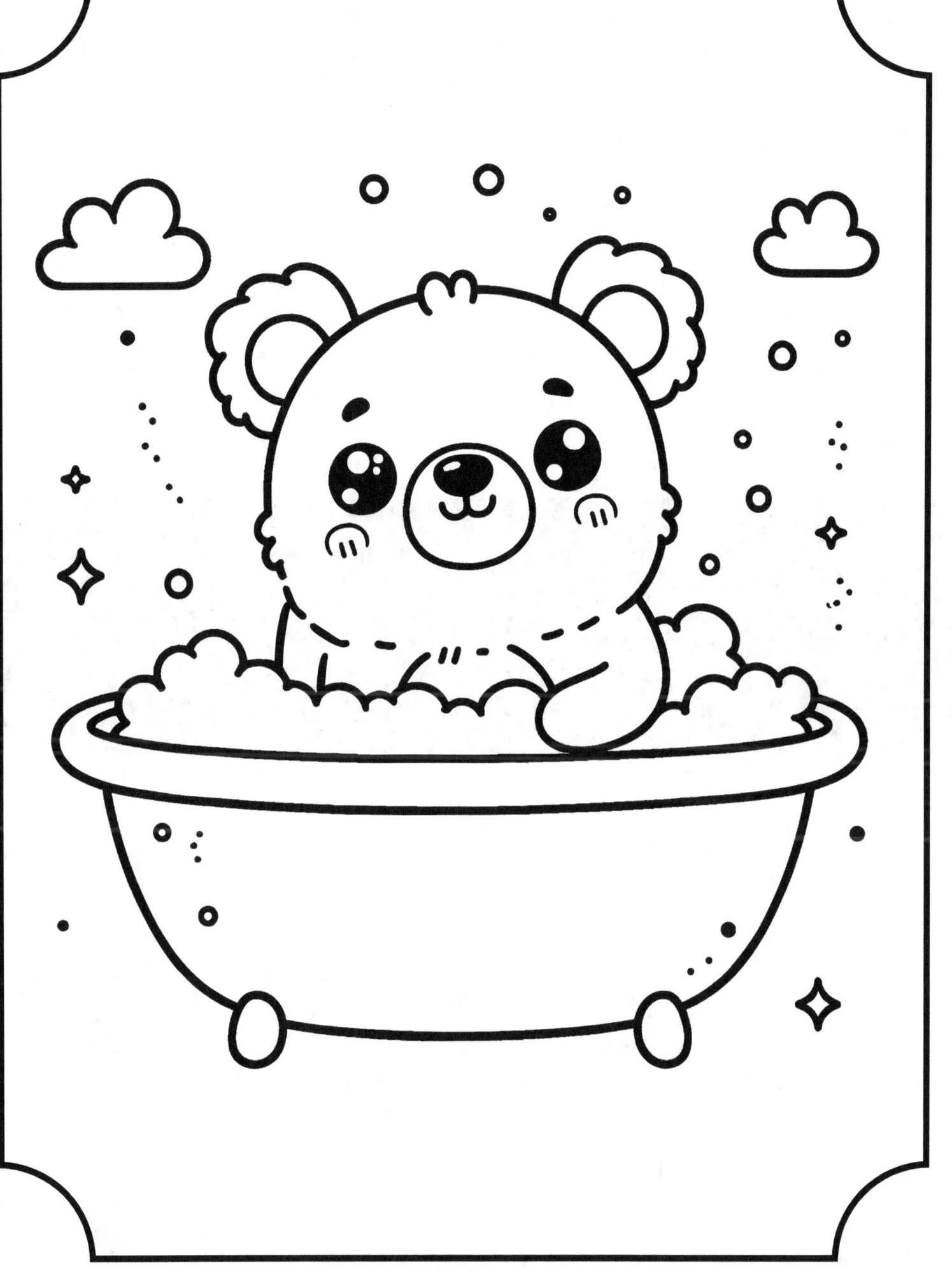

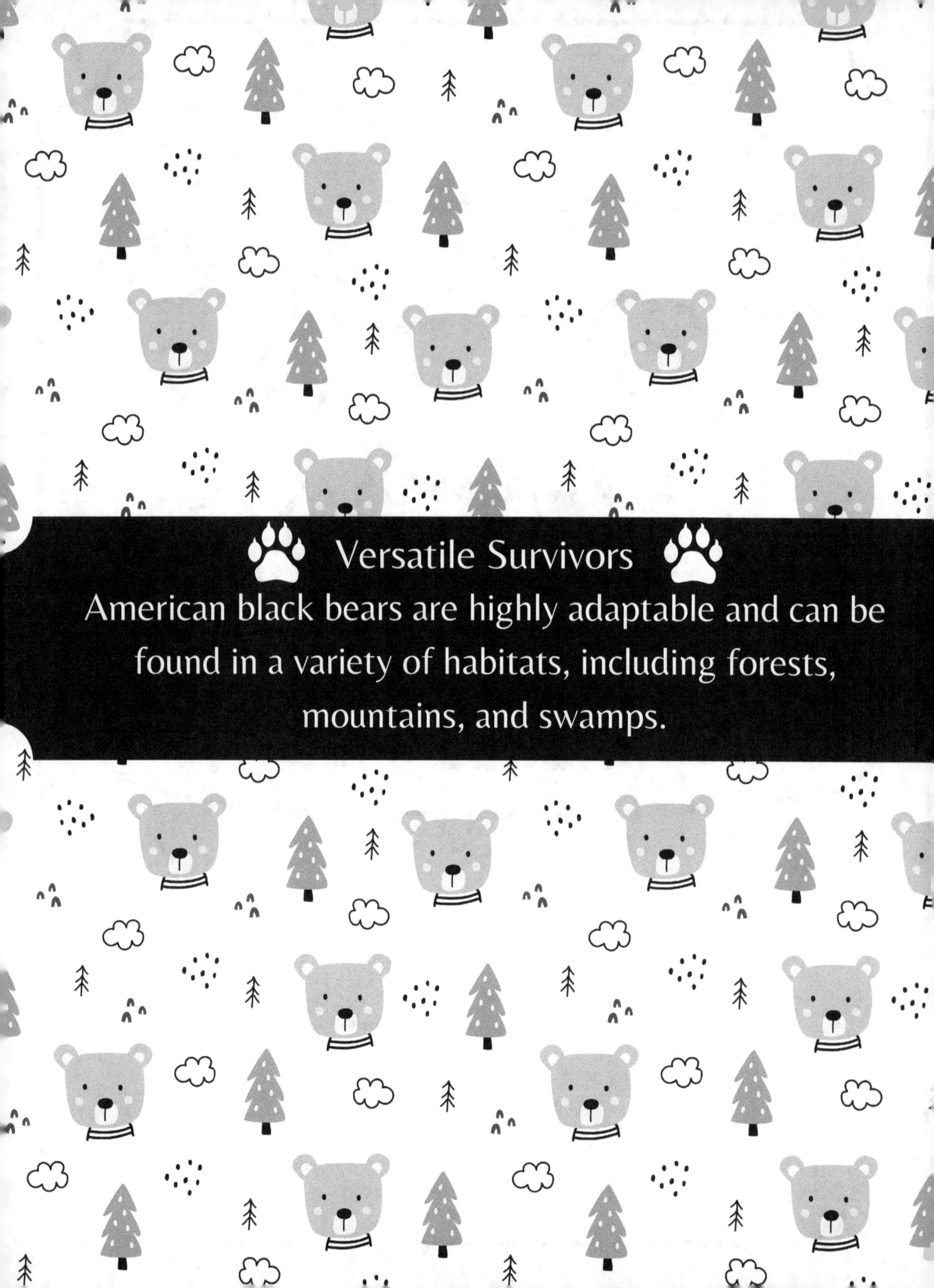

🐾 Versatile Survivors 🐾
American black bears are highly adaptable and can be found in a variety of habitats, including forests, mountains, and swamps.

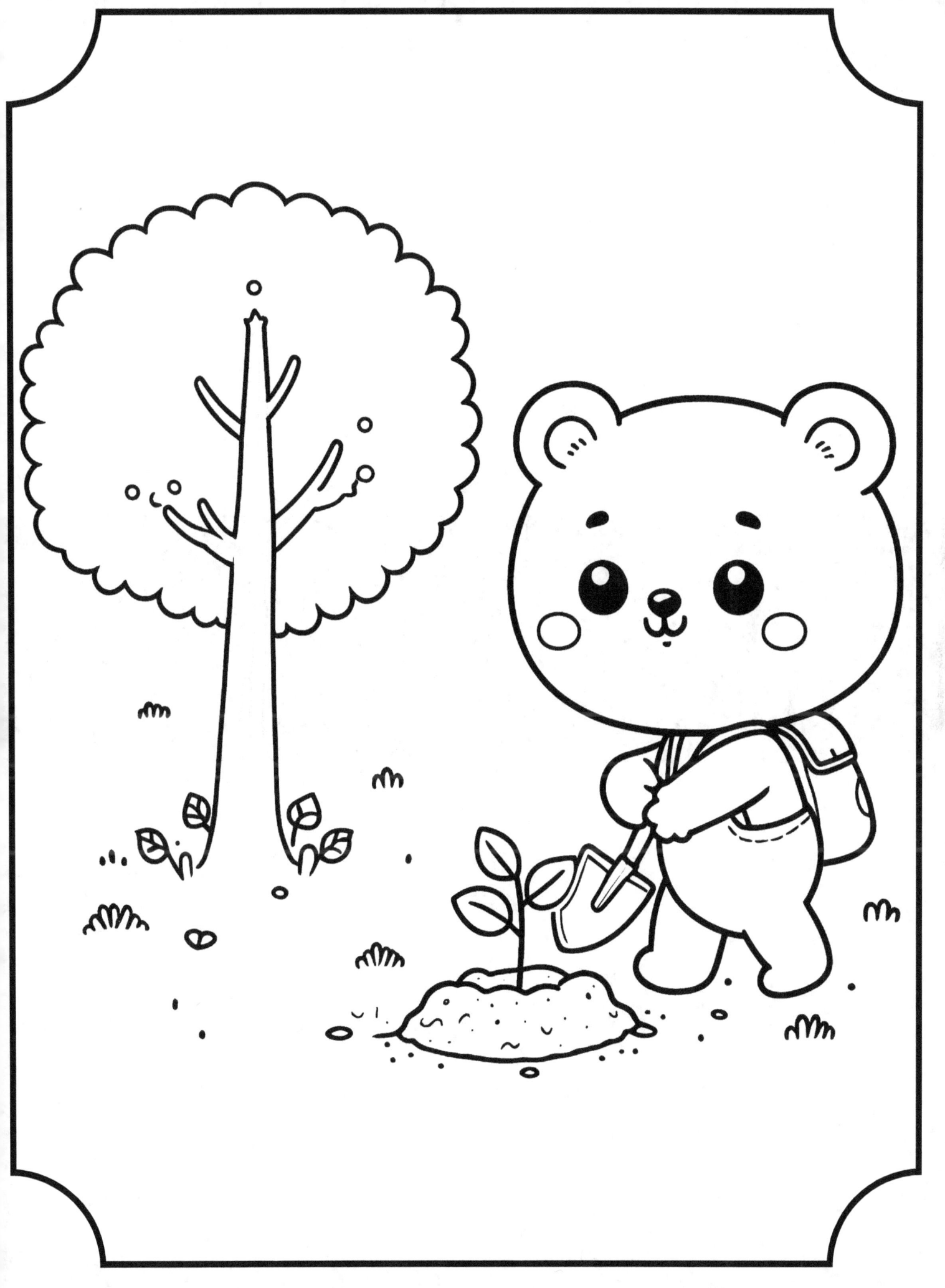

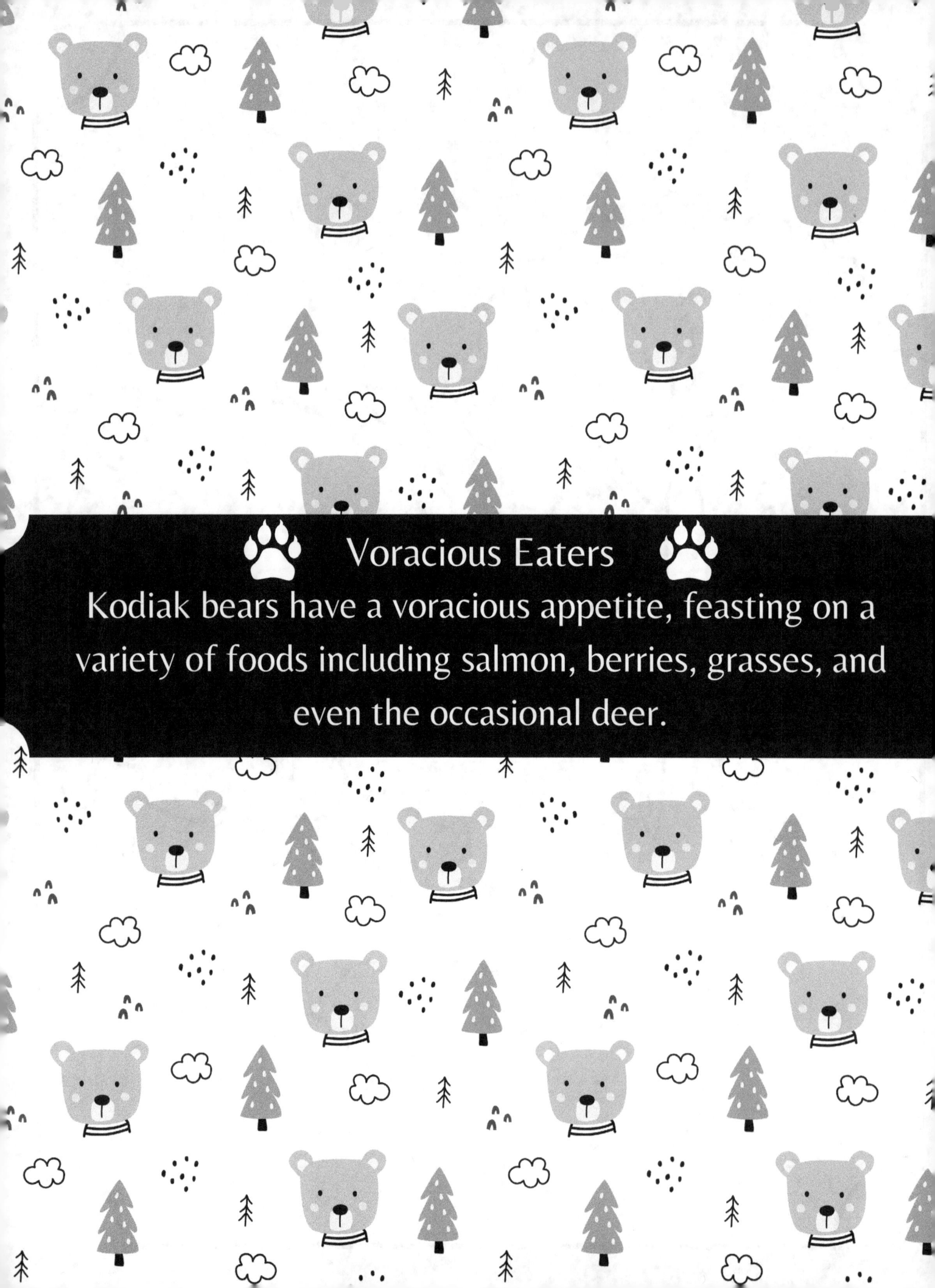

🐾 Voracious Eaters 🐾
Kodiak bears have a voracious appetite, feasting on a variety of foods including salmon, berries, grasses, and even the occasional deer.

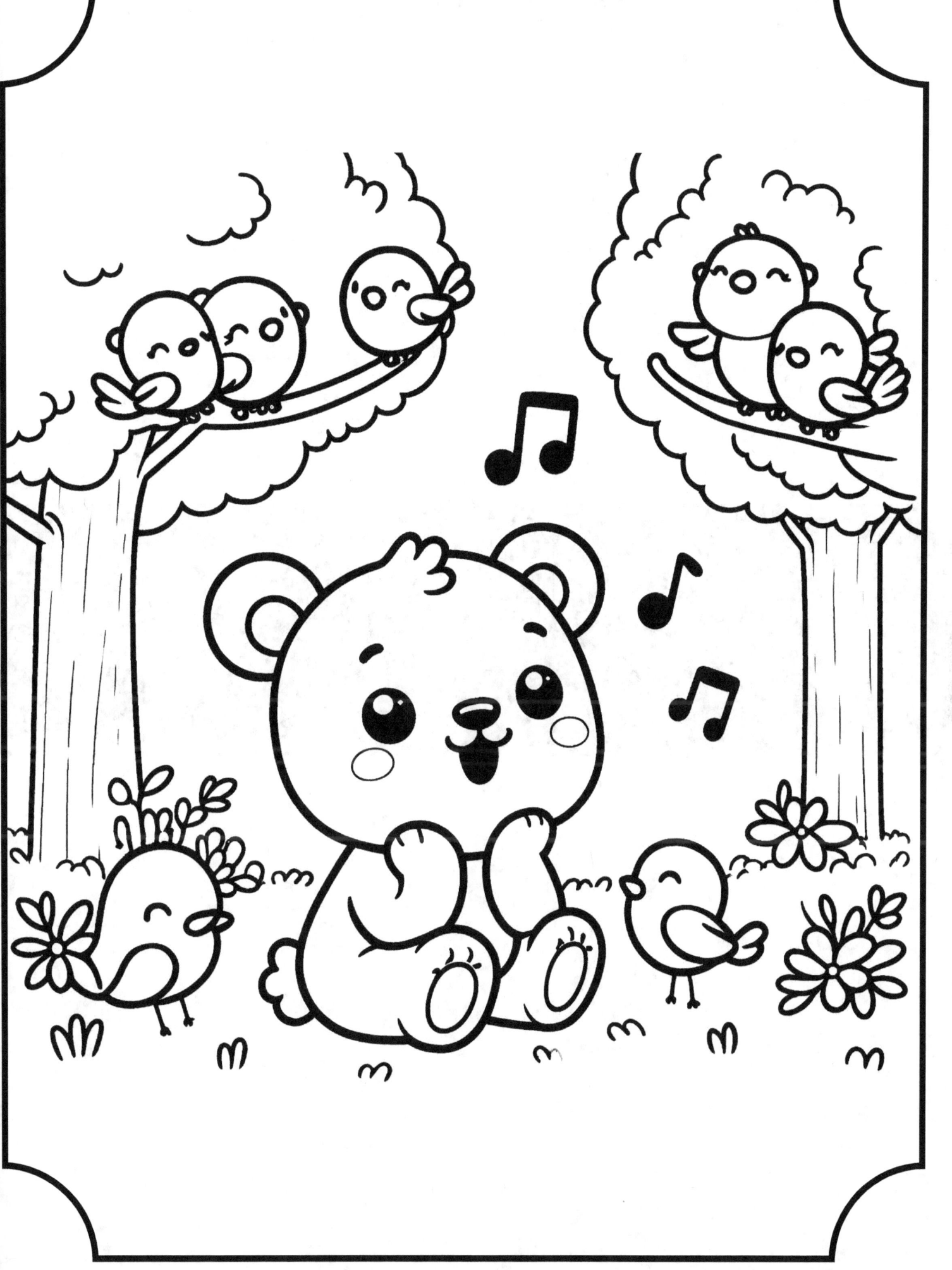

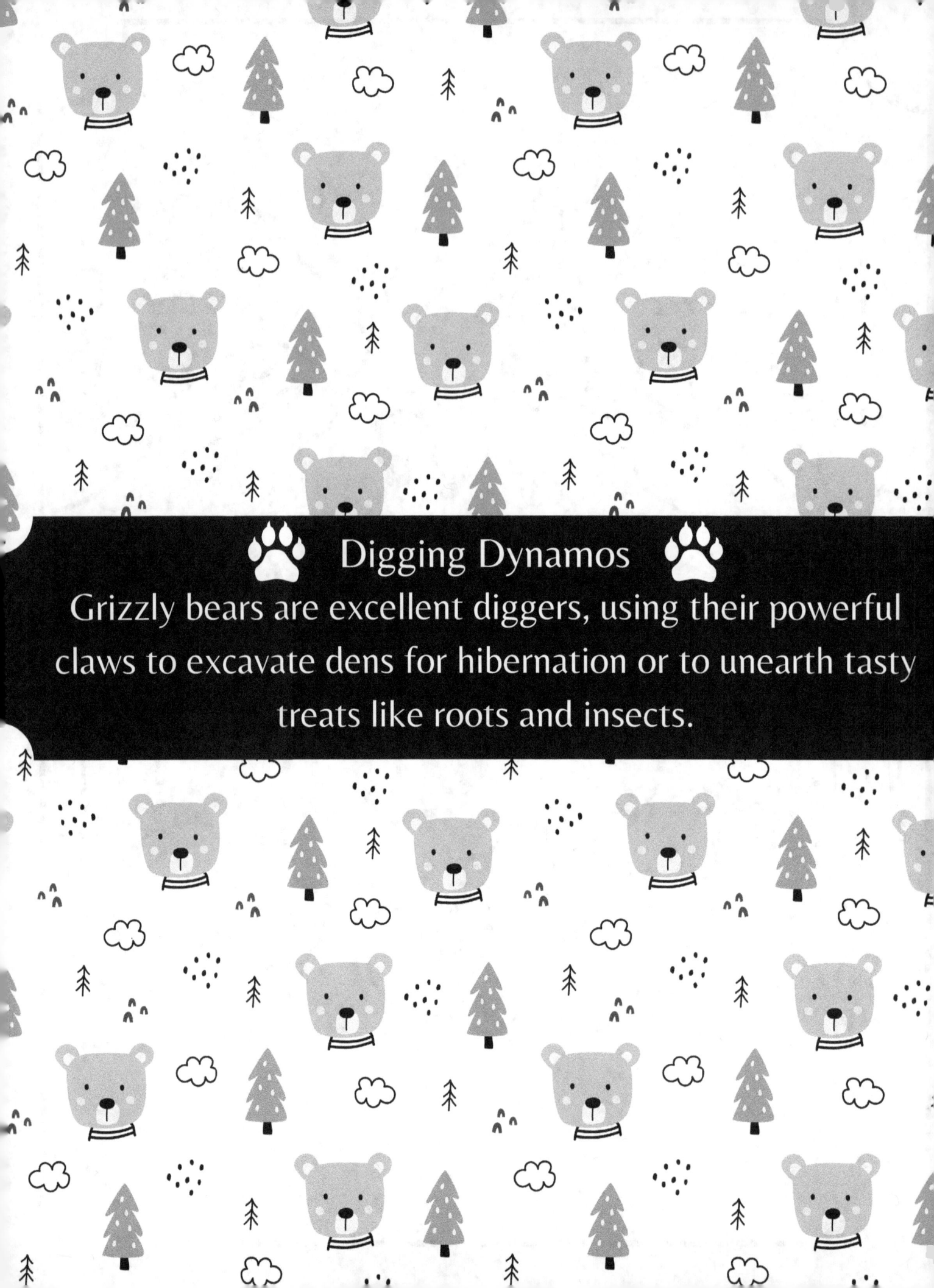

🐾 Digging Dynamos 🐾
Grizzly bears are excellent diggers, using their powerful claws to excavate dens for hibernation or to unearth tasty treats like roots and insects.

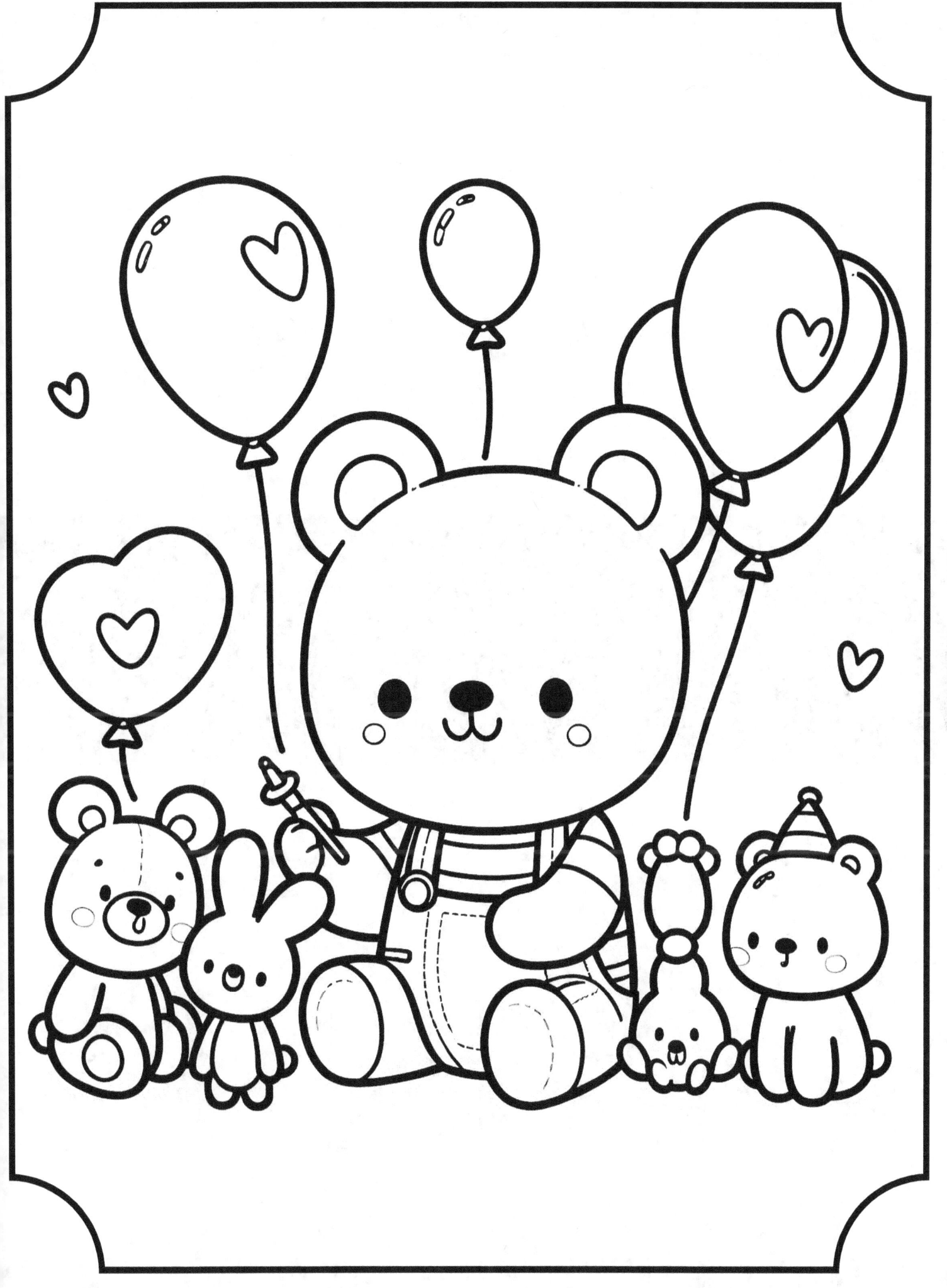

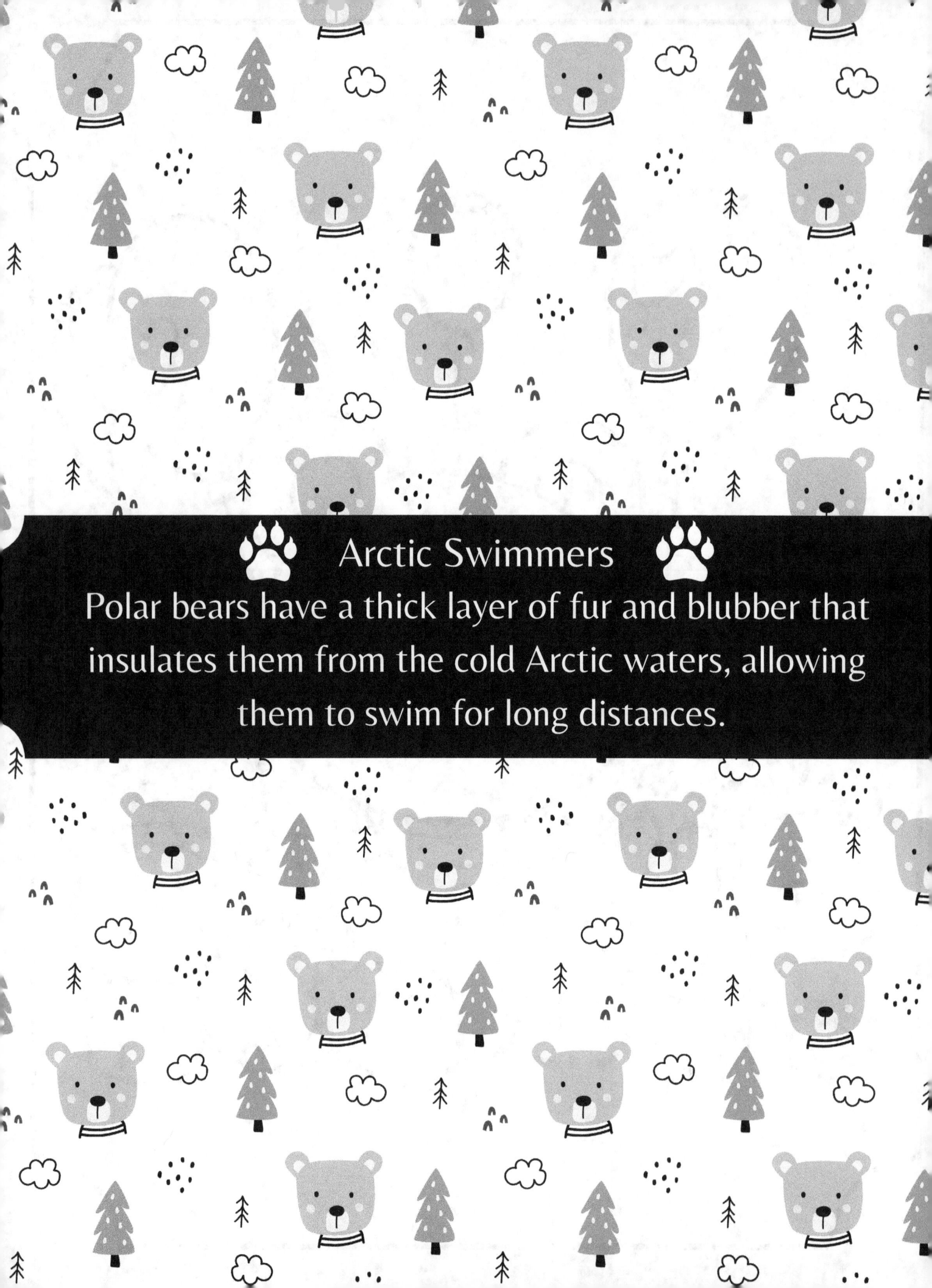

Arctic Swimmers
Polar bears have a thick layer of fur and blubber that insulates them from the cold Arctic waters, allowing them to swim for long distances.

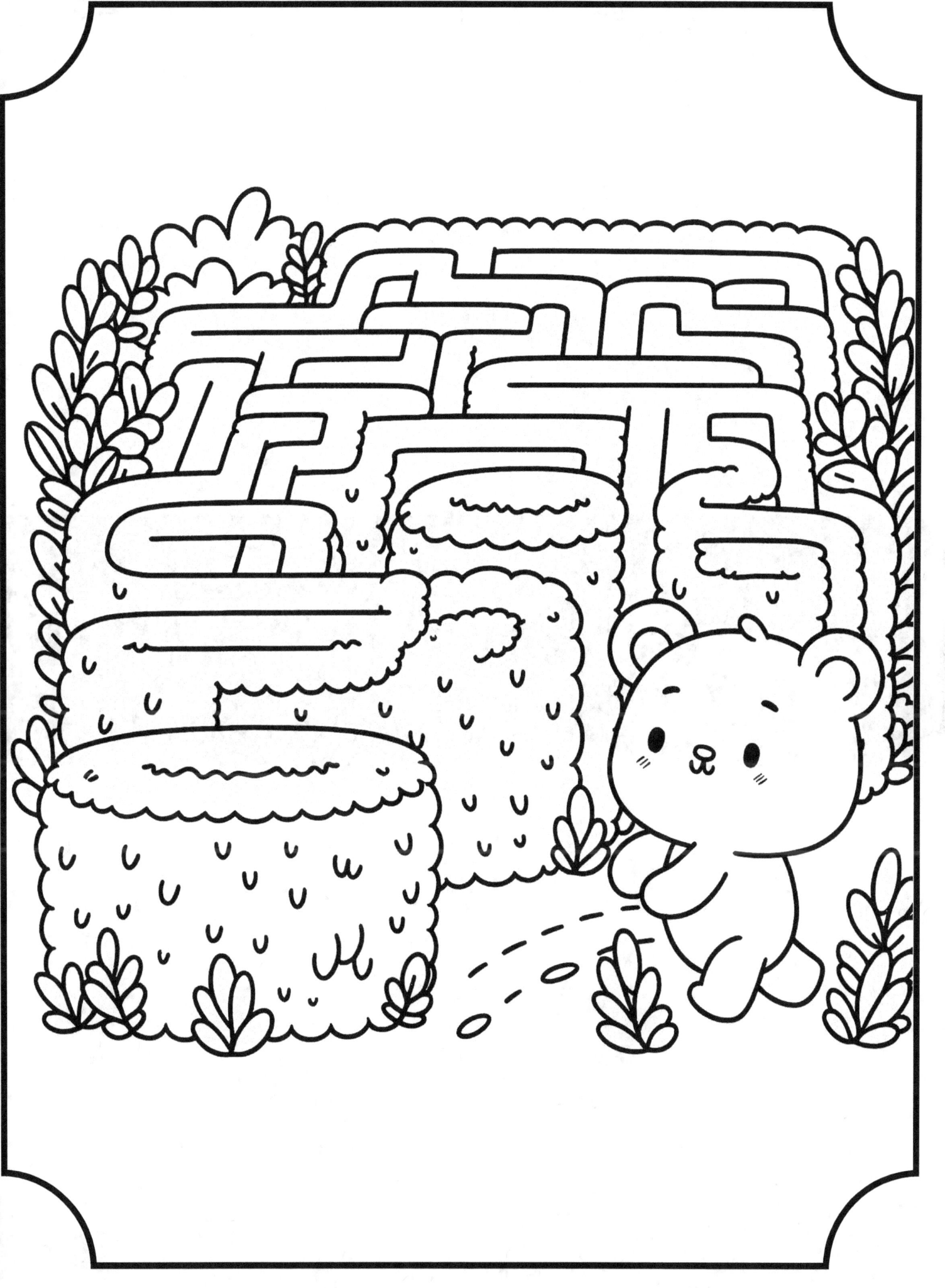

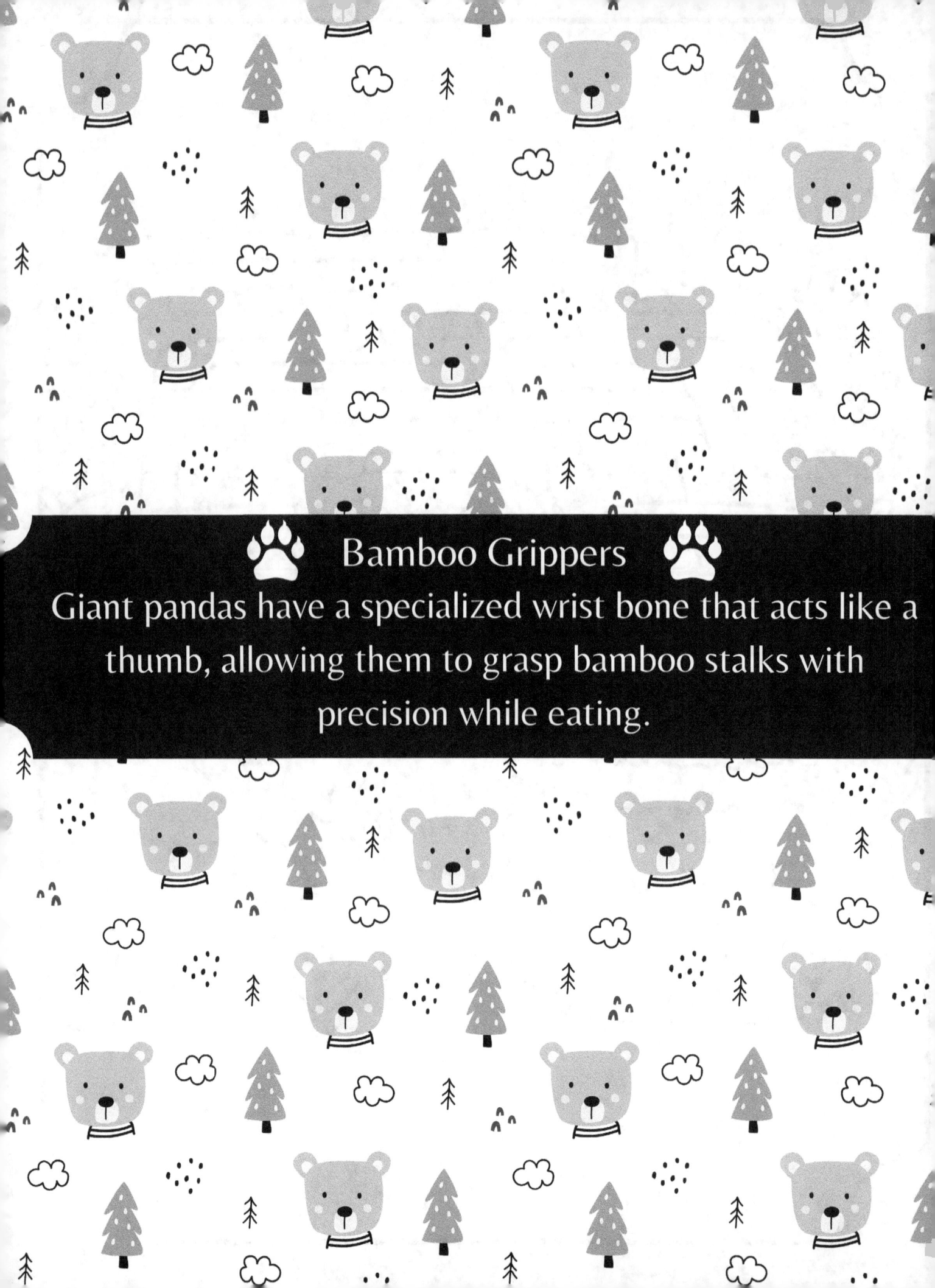

🐾 Bamboo Grippers 🐾
Giant pandas have a specialized wrist bone that acts like a thumb, allowing them to grasp bamboo stalks with precision while eating.

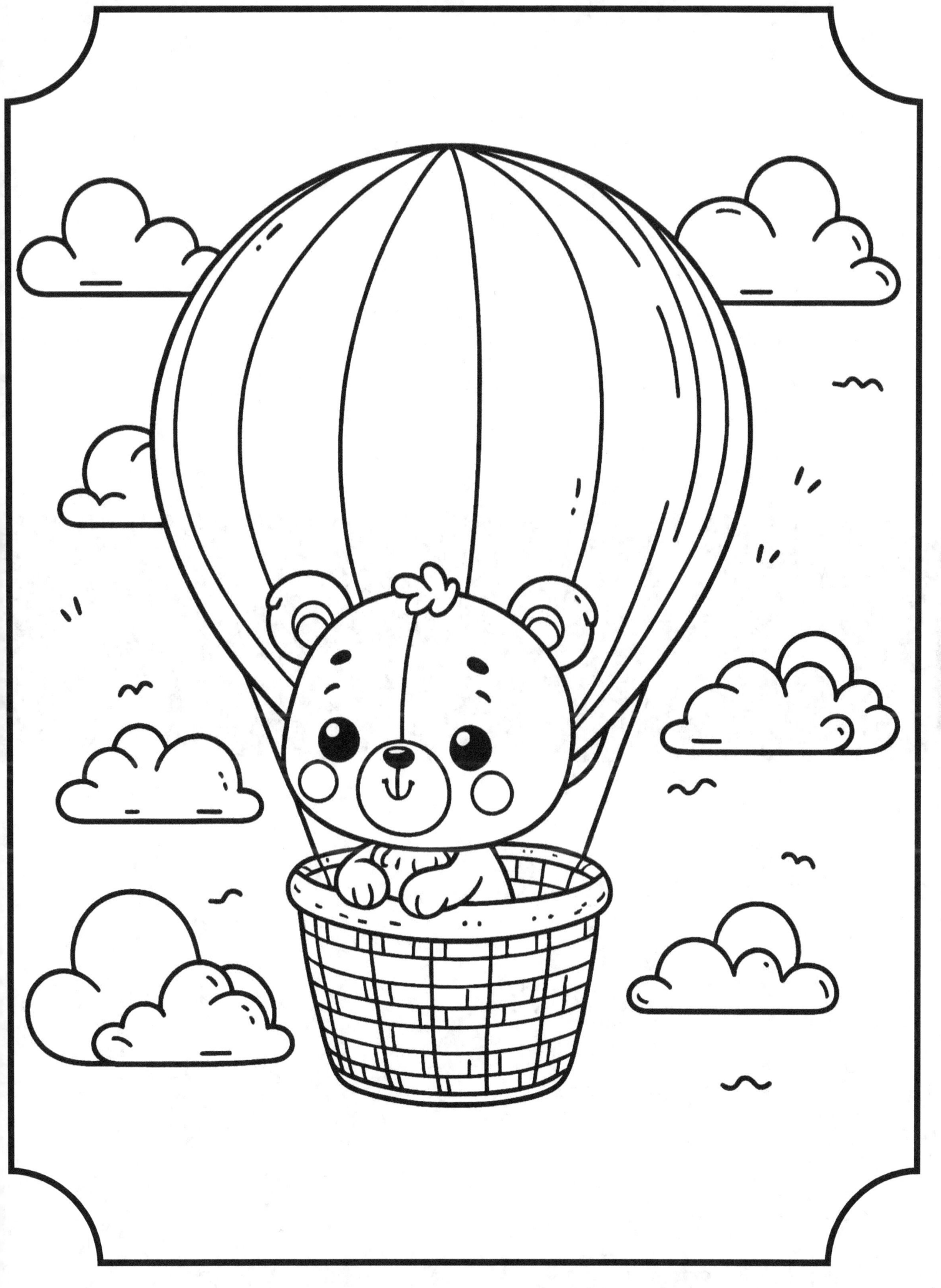

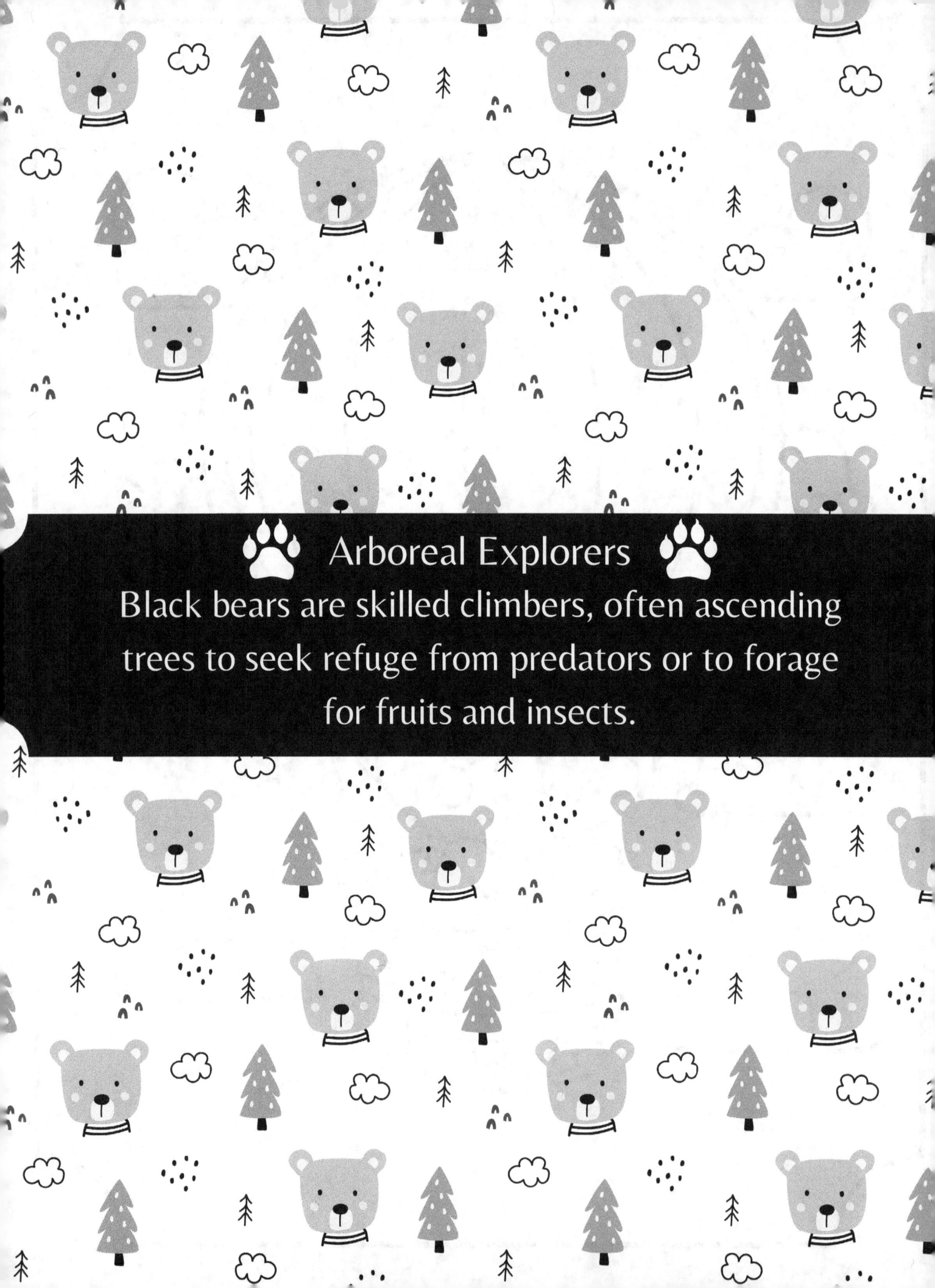

Arboreal Explorers
Black bears are skilled climbers, often ascending trees to seek refuge from predators or to forage for fruits and insects.

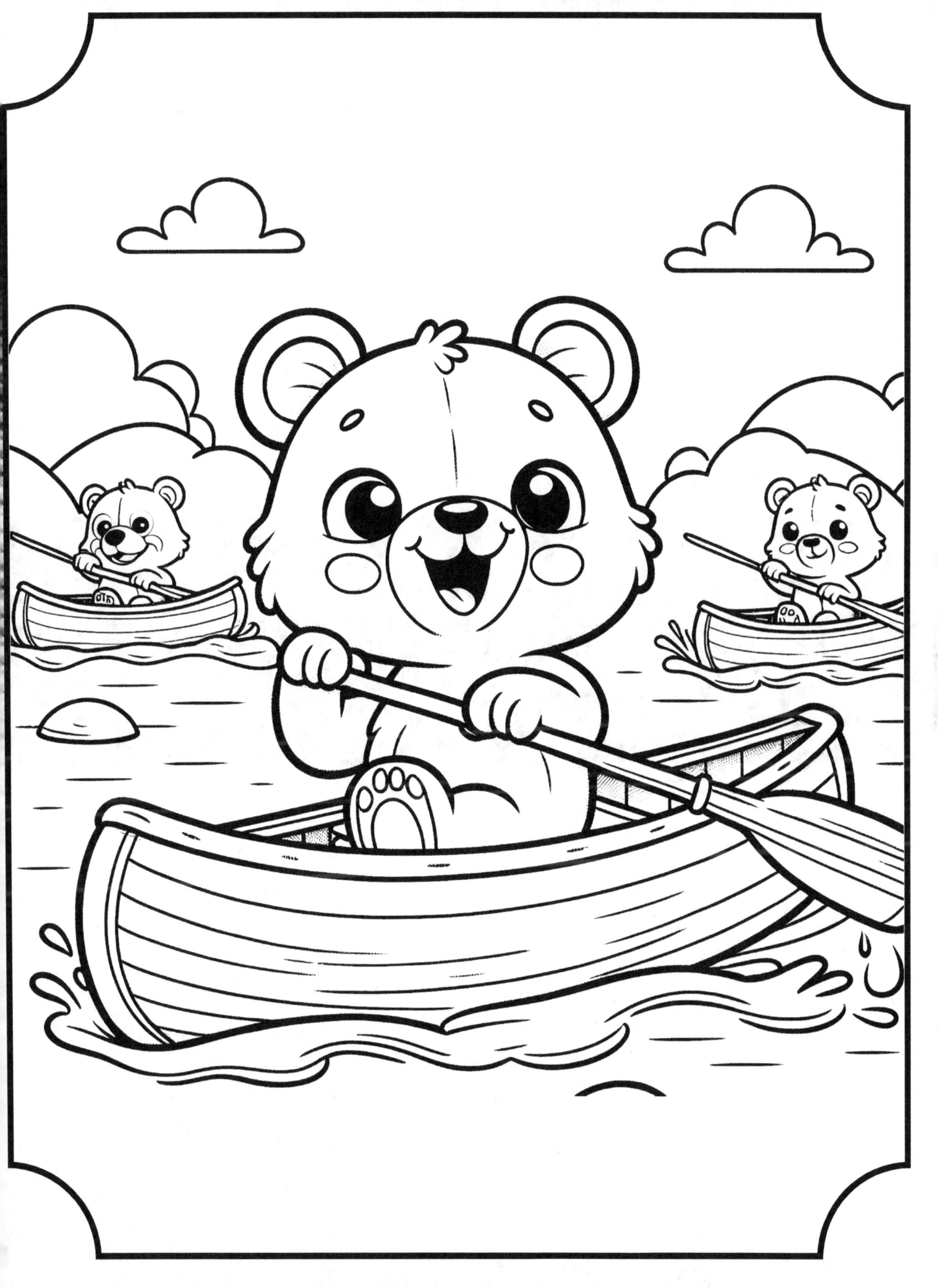

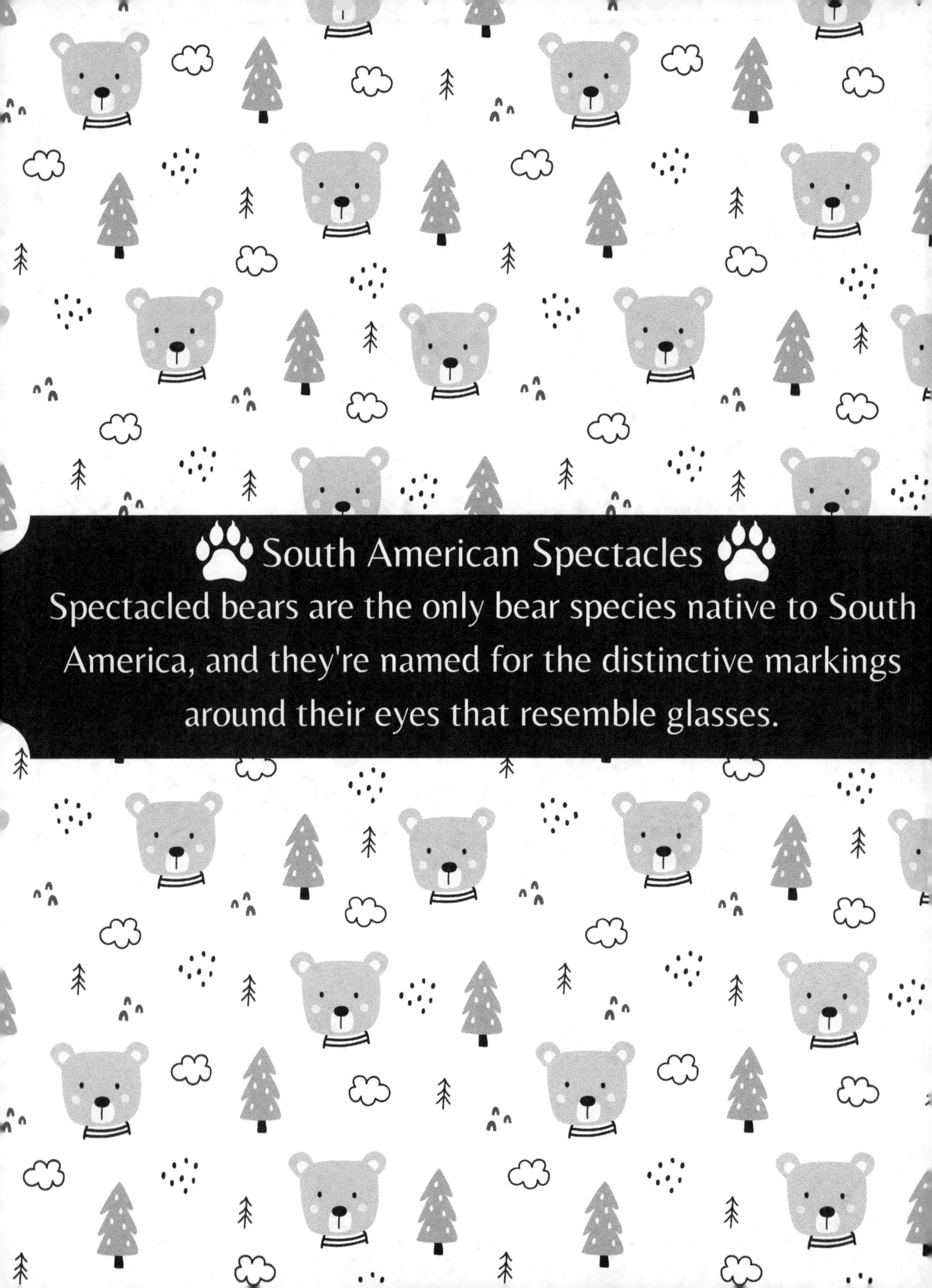

🐾 South American Spectacles 🐾
Spectacled bears are the only bear species native to South America, and they're named for the distinctive markings around their eyes that resemble glasses.

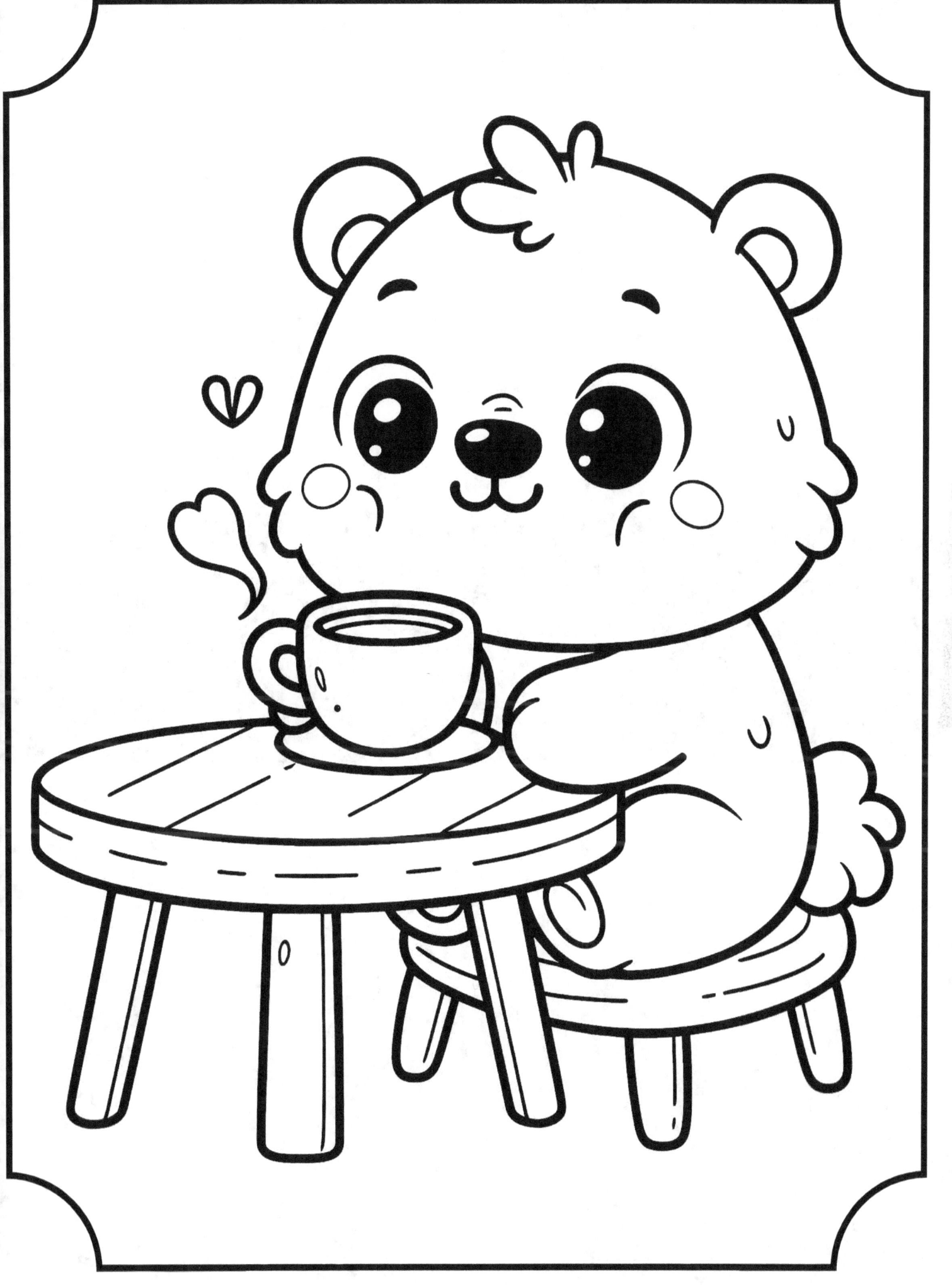

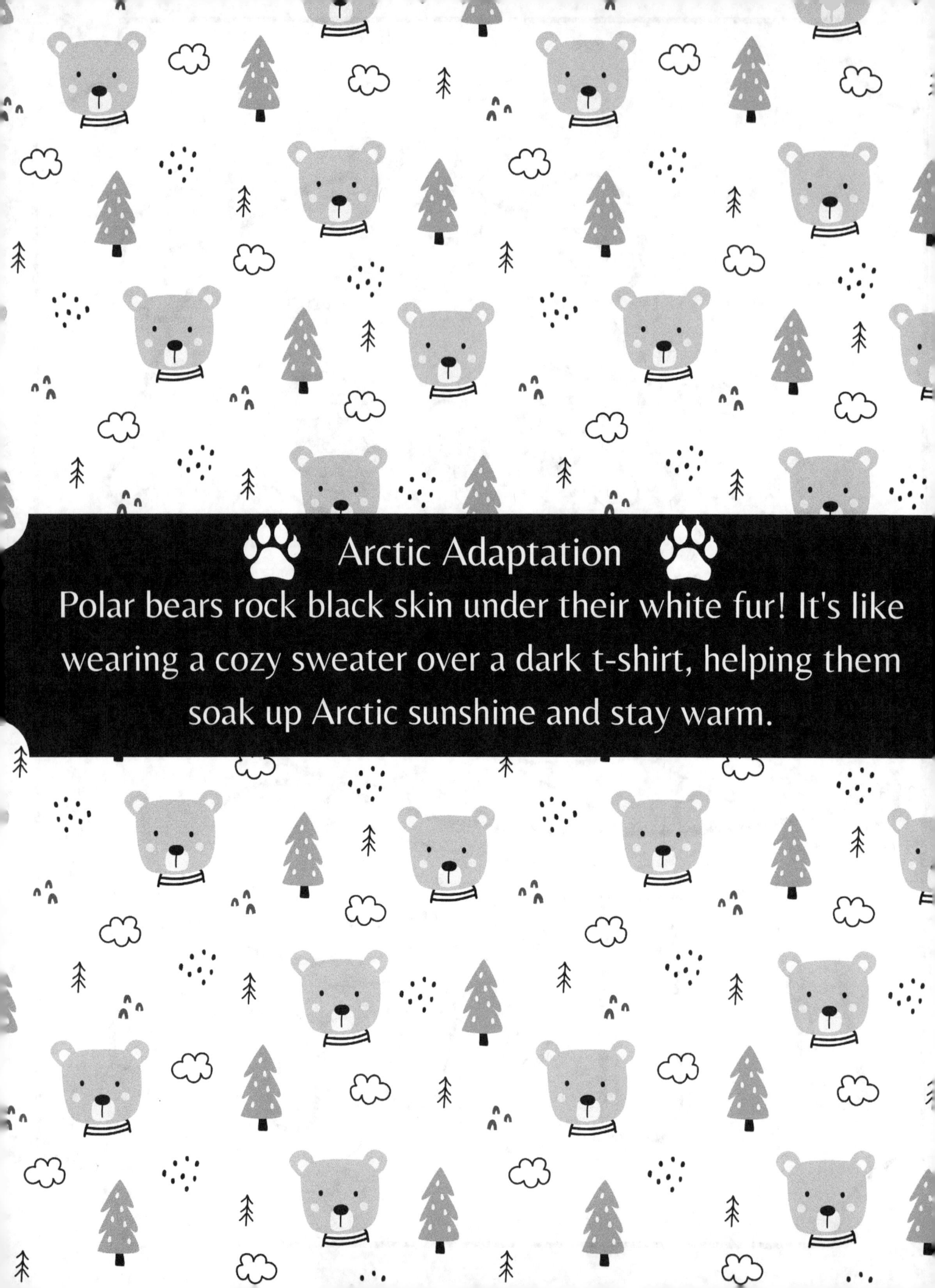

Arctic Adaptation
Polar bears rock black skin under their white fur! It's like wearing a cozy sweater over a dark t-shirt, helping them soak up Arctic sunshine and stay warm.

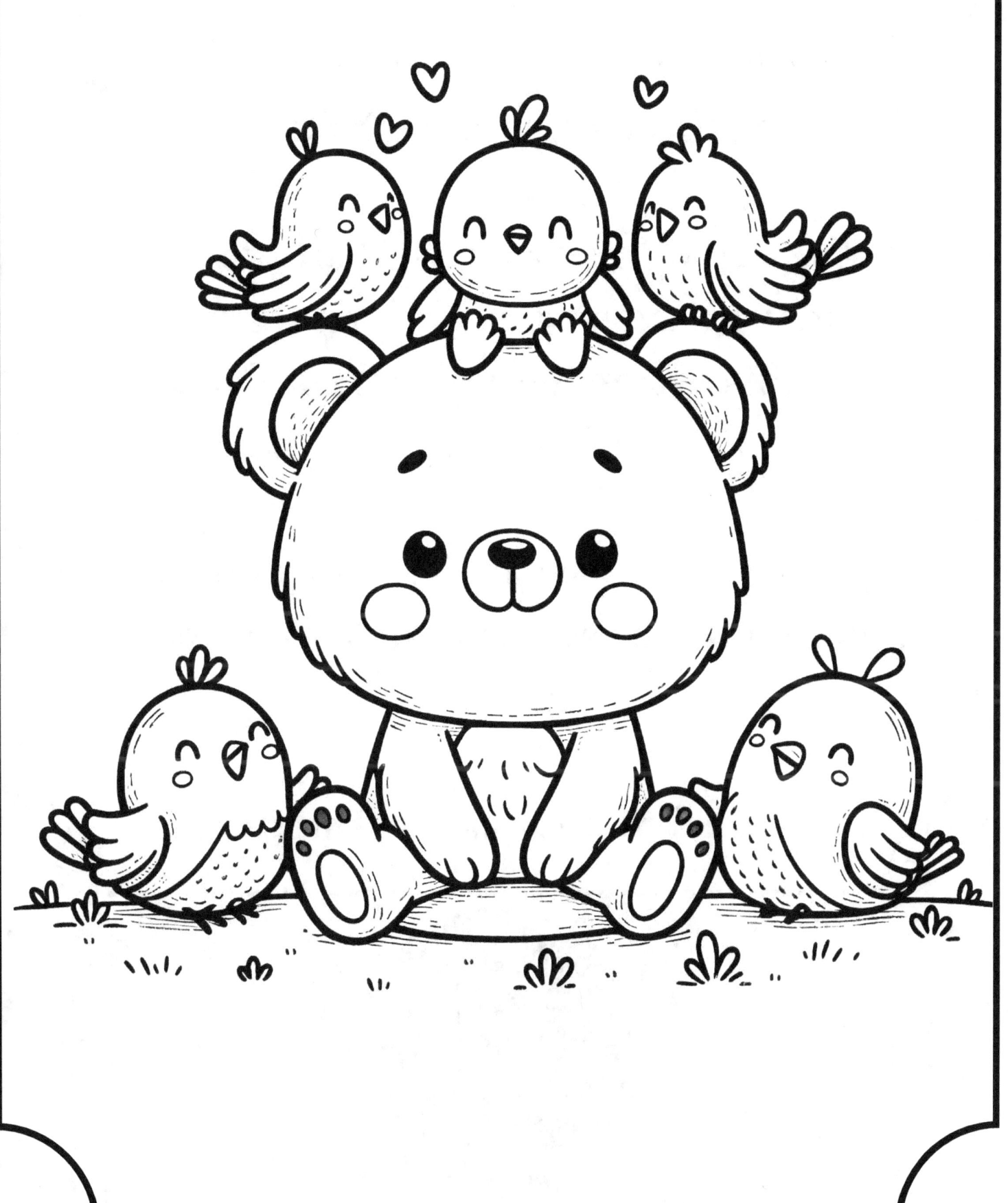

Did you enjoy our book?

Looking for a greater challenge?

If you enjoy our book, we'd love to hear from you! If you want, you can share your thoughts in a review and tell us what kind of activity book you'd like next.

Follow us on social media to stay updated on when we release more special books just for you!

Search for us as **Positive Dungeons**.

Endless gratitude for reaching this point

We want to express our sincerest gratitude for dedicating your time to enjoy our book. We understand that time is a precious resource, and we greatly appreciate the fact that you have chosen to spend some of yours with us.

We would love to hear your thoughts about our book. If you have a quick 50 seconds, we cordially invite you to share your feedback, comments, or any ideas you wish to convey. Your thoughts on what you've garnered from this book are valued and awaited.

Here are the steps to leave your review:

1. Open your mobile camera.
2. Access the link by scanning the QR code below.
3. Follow the link to write your review.

Or visit:

https://condesa07.com/amazonReview/BearColoringBook

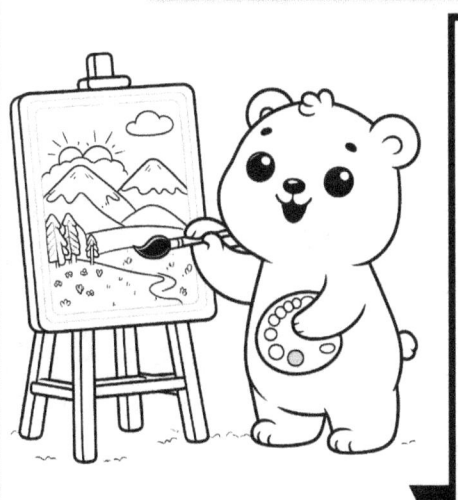

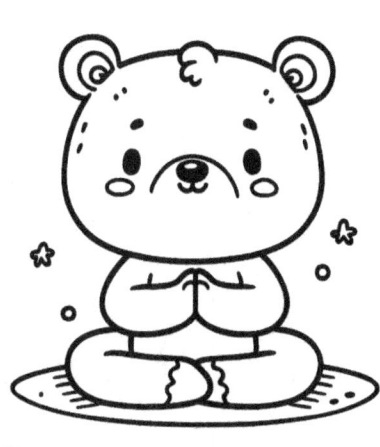

Scan Me!

www.ingramcontent.com/pod-product-compliance
Lightning Source LLC
Chambersburg PA
CBHW082214220526
45470CB00010B/3168